lonely planet

POCKET

JERUSALEM & TEL AVIV

TOP SIGHTS · LOCAL EXPERIENCES

MASOVAIDA MORGAN,
MICHAEL GROSBERG, ANITA ISALSKA

Contents

Plan Your Trip

Al Aqsa Mosque (p36), Jerusalem
ASIM BHARWANI/GETTY IMAGES ©

Explore
Jerusalem 31

Explore
Tel Aviv 109

Worth a Trip

Survival
Guide 169

COVID-19

We have re-checked every business in this book before publication to ensure that it is still open after the COVID-19 outbreak. However, the economic and social impacts of COVID-19 will continue to be felt long after the outbreak has been contained, and many businesses, services and events referenced in this guide may experience ongoing restrictions. Some businesses may be temporarily closed, have changed their opening hours and services, or require bookings; some unfortunately could have closed permanently. We suggest you check with venues before visiting for the latest information.

Top Experiences

**Visit Jerusalem's holiest site:
Temple Mount/Al Haram Ash Sharif (p34)**

See five stations of the cross at Church of the Holy Sepulchre (p38)

Tour the tunnels under the Western Wall (p42)

Watch some *matkot* on Tel Aviv's Beaches (p156)

Pay your respects at Yad Vashem's Holocaust memorials (p102)

Find an antique treasure at Jaffa Flea Market (p160)

See a piece of the original Dead Sea Scrolls at the Israel Museum (p92)

Take a tasting tour of Mahane Yehuda Market (p76)

Catch a film or show at the Tel Aviv Museum of Art (p112)

Try the best *boureka* in town at Carmel Market (p130)

Get active in Park HaYarkon (p148)

Dining Out

DANIEL REINER/SHUTTERSTOCK ©

From traditional Middle Eastern and Mediterranean to Franco-Israeli fusion, Jerusalem and Tel Aviv are a food-lover's delight, with hole-in-the-wall eateries, trendy bistros and high-end restaurants that would give any European city a run for its money.

Eating in Jerusalem

The two tent poles of Middle Eastern street food, falafel and hummus, are available at every turn, and cooking with seasonal and local ingredients goes without saying. Staples like aubergine, chickpeas, olives, dates, parsley and fragrant *zaatar* (a blend of spices that includes hyssop, sumac and sesame) prop up the traditional and bring new perspectives to the burgeoning international scene.

Eating in Tel Aviv

Smack bang in the middle of the Middle East, this cuisine has Mediterranean, Balkan, Arab and Asian influences. Tel Aviv is also one of the most vegan-friendly cities on earth. There really is something for all tastes, from seafood to Greek-inspired restaurants, Asian eateries and Italian joints.

Kosher Restaurants

Israeli law does not require restaurants to be kosher – it's up to the owner to arrange (and pay for) kosher certification by the local Rabbinate branch. Kosher restaurants, which must close on Shabbat and Jewish holidays, are almost always either *basari* (*fleishig* in Yiddish; 'meat') or *chalavi* (*milchig* in Yiddish; 'dairy', ie vegetarian plus fish). Most Jewish restaurants in West Jerusalem are kosher, except for those in hotels, which means that it can be hard to find a place to eat on Shabbat, as most places shut up shop on Friday afternoon and reopen on Saturday evening.

FOTOKON/SHUTTERSTOCK ©

Best Fine Dining

Machneyuda Always-busy place (pictured above right) serving playful haute cuisine. (p84)

Dalida Arab, Italian and French cuisines come together with class. (p138)

Taizu High-class Asian fusion with top notch service. (p137)

Anna Simple but impeccably prepared fish and Italian fare in an airy 19th-century villa. (p84)

Best Middle Eastern

Port Sa'id Middle Eastern–inspired menu that draws a hip crowd. (p138)

Modern Contemporary Israeli cuisine with a Sephardic twist in an artistically designed setting. (p93)

Miznon Stuffed-pita perfection in a high energy atmosphere. (p119)

Azura Bubbling kerosene cauldrons of Iraqi specialties. (p84)

Best Vegetarian & Vegan

Meshek Barzilay One of the best vegan breakfasts in Tel Aviv. (p139)

Best Hummus & Falafel

Abu Kamel They hand-crush the chickpeas at this hard-to-find Old City spot. (p53)

Beit Lechem Hummus Florentin's favourite – try yours topped with a fried egg. (p140)

HaKosem Friendly falafel stand that's popular with the local crowd. (p120)

Abu Shukri No menu, just legendary hummus and sparking imitators. (p53)

Bar Open

From Jerusalem's wine bars to beers on the beach and partying all night in Tel Aviv, you'll find a well-established drinking culture. When it comes to clubbing, bars with dancing and live gigs dominate the scene. The big night out is Thursday, with Fridays far quieter because of Shabbat.

Nightlife in Jerusalem

Jerusalem's downtown is well endowed with bars. The best are in the Mahane Yehuda Market area and in the vicinity of Zion Sq, on Rivlin, Ben Shatah, Hillel, Heleni HaMalka and Dorot Rishonim Sts. East Jerusalem bars tend to be inside hotels, while the Old City is almost as dry as the Negev desert.

Nightlife in Tel Aviv

With craft beer breweries, wine bars, quirky dives and picturesque rooftops, a good drink in Tel Aviv is never far from reach. Some spots are pumping, others so chilled they're almost comatose. For relaxed, jovial vibes, hit Dizengoff St in the City Centre or head south to Florentin. Rothschild Blvd and Allenby St is also a sure bet.

Club Dress Code

Dress codes are relaxed – you can enter almost any pub or club in sport shoes or sandals (some places may object to thongs/flip flops). It's not unusual to see people out in tank tops, shorts or bikinis in the summer.

Craft Beers

For decades the market was dominated by Tempo (which makes Goldstar and Maccabi), but that's since changed. Local boutique brews such as Malka (wheat beer), Alexander (amber or black stout), Taybeh (a rare beer brewed in the Palestinian Territories) and Dancing Camel (made in Tel Aviv) are proudly stocked.

FOTOKON/SHUTTERSTOCK ©

Best Cocktails

223 Tel Aviv's first cocktail bar, pouring classic libations in a cosy space. (p154)

Spicehaus Pharmacy-inspired concept bar with concoctions as tasty as they are quirky. (p121)

Gatsby's Cocktail Room Some of Jerusalem's best cocktails in a jazzy space. (p89)

Barood Local wine, cocktails and delicious Balkan-meets-Italian nibbles (p87)

Best Rooftops

Prince Once a well-kept secret, this inviting joint draws a large but chilled crowd. (p142)

Kanta Trendy urban garden oasis near Rabin Square. (p121)

Garden Terrace Waldorf Astoria's classy roof lounge with Old City views. (p89)

Mamilla Rooftop Restaurant Close-up views of Jaffa Gate–area walls from this sleek brasserie. (p86)

Best Wine Bars

Talbiye Intimate bistro for a casual drink or date under the Jerusalem Theatre. (p100)

Hashchena Wine Bar Loud and overflowing, with a wide range of wines and cocktails. (p89)

Best Clubs

Alphabet The dance floors may be smaller than other clubs, but the beats definitely aren't. (p142)

Kuli Alma Plenty of chill outdoor spaces – plus an art gallery – when you need a breather from the dance floor. (p141)

Treasure Hunt

Given the huge number of religious pilgrims that pass through the country, Israel is great for souvenirs. You'll find fantastic markets, fashionable boutiques, hole-in-the-wall antique haunts, artisans' shops, behemoth malls, and your pick of unique jewellery by homegrown designers.

Shopping in Jerusalem

Jerusalem is an excellent place to shop for religious souvenirs: browse the Cardo (p50) and various souqs in the Old City or downtown's Yo'el Salomon St, but avoid David St, where products are generally of inferior quality. Elsewhere, best buys include delicate Armenian ceramics and foodie souvenirs from the Muslim Quarter and Mahane Yehuda Market (p76).

Shopping in Tel Aviv

Tel Aviv isn't quite a fashion capital, though there are great small, homegrown labels and jewellery designers. You'll pay more than average for clothing and shoes from mass market retailers – money is much better spent on one-of-a-kind pieces at the boutiques in the Jaffa Flea Market, along Shabazi St in Neve Tzedek and on Sheinkin St in the city centre.

Best Markets

Mahane Yehuda Market Whether it's fresh fish or artisan beer, 'the shuk', as it's called in Hebrew, has it all. (p76)

Jaffa Flea Market Vintage, antiques and chic boutiques pepper the ancient streets. (p160)

Carmel Market One-stop shop for cheap wares, fresh produce and tasty street food. (p130)

Sarona Upmarket shops and charming cafes in Templer structures. (p124; pictured above)

INNAFELKER/SHUTTERSTOCK ©

Best Judaica

Greenvurcel Stylish, contemporary Judaica metalwork. (p91)

Moriah Books & Judaica One stop shop for Talmuds to menorahs in the Old City's Jewish Quarter. (p57)

Heifetz Contemporary designs for traditional Jewish ritual items and jewellery. (p57)

Best Art & Design

Nahalat Binyamin Crafts Market Handmade wares, jewellery and more by Tel Aviv's creative contingent. (p144)

Dauhaus Centre Architecture-inspired books and souvenirs. (p125)

Saga Modern gallery and shop showcasing the works of local talent. (p166)

Artists' Colony Galleries for ceramics, paintings, metalwork and Judaica lining a cobblestone street. (p90)

Mango Tree Design-your-own necklaces and more at fair prices. (p125)

Best Ceramics

EK Ceramic Fixed-priced floral designs sold in an Old City souq for generations. (p56)

Arman Daria Ceramic One of the Jerusalem's best-known ceramicists selling small and large pieces. (p91)

Best Fashion

Kikar HaMedina Posh designer retailers rule this roundabout. (p155)

History

Layers of history continue to be un-earthed in Jerusalem, where ancient worlds are tantalisingly close – hardly a month goes by without a significant discovery being made in and around the Old City. For thousands of years, while Tel Aviv was nothing more than dunes, Jaffa stood as one of the great ports of the Mediterranean.

Ancient Jaffa

According to archae-ologists, Jaffa was a fortified port at least as far back as the 18th century BC. An Egyptian document from around 1470 BC mentions the city's conquest by Pharaoh Tuthmosis III.

The ancient Israelite port of 'Joppa' (as mentioned in the Hebrew Bible) came to prominence dur-ing the reign of King Solomon, while the temple was being built in Jerusalem. Over the centuries, Jaffa was conquered by, among others, the Assyrians (701 BC), the Babylonians (586 BC), Alexander the Great (332 BC), the Egyptians (301 BC) and the Maccabees (mid-1st century BC), but was neglected by the Romans, who had their own port up the coast at Caesarea. In Greek mythology, An-dromeda was chained to a rock just off the coast of Jaffa.

The New City of Tel Aviv

In 1906, 60 Jewish families laid out plans to establish an entire-ly new city. They pur-chased 12.8 hectares of empty sand dunes north of Jaffa, divided it into 60 lots and held a lottery – using seashells – to divvy up the land around what is now the in-tersection of Herzl St and Rothschild Blvd. They took as a model the English 'garden city' (a planned, self-contained com-munity with plenty of public parks and open spaces). By the time WWI broke out in 1914, 140 homes had been built.

The name of the new city, Tel Aviv (Hill of Spring), comes from the title of the Hebrew translation of

TOWER OF DAVID (P48): SEAN PAVONE/SHUTTERSTOCK ©

Theodor Herzl's utopian novel *Altneuland*; it's also mentioned in Ezekiel 3:15.

First Temple

Jerusalem's earliest settlements surrounded the Gihon Spring, in the Kidron Valley just southeast of the present-day Jewish Quarter. A small Canaanite city is mentioned in Egyptian texts of the 20th century BC, and biblical sources say it was conquered around 1000 BC by the Israelites under King David, who made the city his capital.

Biblical sources say that, under King Solomon (David's son), the boundaries of the city were extended north to enclose the spur of land that is now Temple Mount/Al Haram Ash Sharif. The construction of the First Temple began around 950 BC.

Best Archaeology in Jerusalem

Western Wall Tunnels Learn about King Herod's building tricks on a subterranean guided tour of the Western Wall (p43)

City of David Jerusalem's ancient corners continue to be unearthed at this active (and deeply controversial) dig. (p66)

Rockefeller Museum Uncrowded castle-like building filled with significant archaeological finds. (p68)

Terra Sancta Museum Showcasing Franciscan excavations from Canaanite to Crusader periods, on the grounds of a Via Dolorosa stop. (p49)

Jerusalem Archaeological Park Grab an audio guide and ramble the excavated remains of 2000-year-old streets. (p48)

Architecture

Even as Jerusalem hurtles towards the future, the past informs its present. Downtown's modern buildings are encased in rosy Jerusalem stone, the same colour palette as the Old City. Declared a Unesco World Heritage Site in 2003, Tel Aviv's 'White City' has more Bauhaus-style buildings than anywhere in the world.

Jerusalem's Mamluk Architecture

The Muslim Quarter possesses a wealth of buildings constructed during the golden age of Islamic architecture. This part of the Old City was developed during the era of the Mamluks (1250–1517), a military dynasty of former slaves ruling out of Egypt. Driving the Crusaders out of Palestine and Syria, they consolidated Islam's presence in the Levant by constructing masses of mosques, *madrassas* (religious schools), hostels, monasteries and mausoleums.

Mamluk buildings are characterised by the banding of dark and light stone (a technique known as *ablaq*) and by elaborate carvings and patterning around windows and in recessed portals.

Tel Aviv's Bauhaus Heritage

Tel Aviv's White-City heritage is easy to spot, even through the modifications of the past 70 years. Look for structures characterised by horizontal lines, flat roofs, white walls and an almost complete absence of ornamentation.

Bauhaus was an influential art and design school active in the German cities of Weimar, Dessau and Berlin from 1919 to 1933. The Nazis detested the Bauhaus style and forced the school to close when they came to power.

The modernist ideas and ideals of Bauhaus were brought to Palestine by German-Jewish architects fleeing Nazi persecution. As

HOTEL CINEMA, DESIGNED BY YEHUDA MAGIDOVITCH; PHOTOGRAPHER: PYURY LEDENTSOV/SHUTTERSTOCK ©

Tel Aviv developed in the 1930s, some 4000 white-painted Bauhaus buildings – the quintessence of mid-20th-century modernism – were built. Approximately 1000 of these are identified in the Unesco listing.

War & the Birth of Bauhaus

Tel Aviv's development ground to a halt during WWI, and in the spring of 1917 the Ottoman administration expelled the entire Jewish population from Tel Aviv and Jaffa. After WWI,

the British Mandate in Palestine made it possible for the city to resume its exponential growth. Arab riots in Jaffa in 1921 sent many Jews fleeing north to Tel Aviv, bringing the new city's population to around 34,000 by 1925.

The 1930s saw waves of new arrivals, many fleeing Nazi Germany. A boycott of Jewish passengers and cargo by Jaffa's Arab port workers, begun in 1936, led Tel Aviv to build its very own port. By 1939 Tel Aviv's population had reached 160,000; meanwhile, a few kilo-

metres to the north-east in the Templer settlement of Sarona, the patriotically German residents were flying the Nazi flag.

Jewish architects who had fled Nazi Germany set about designing apartment houses in the clean-lined, modernist Bauhaus style that would soon become the city's hallmark.

Best of Bauhaus

Bauhaus Centre Browse a variety of architecture-related books and plans of the city, plus two Bauhaus walking-tour offerings. (p125)

LGBTIQ+

LGBTIQ+ people pursue an open lifestyle in Tel Aviv, which has plenty of hang-outs, rainbow-coloured flags and a huge Pride Parade. Jerusalem's scene is more low-key. Orthodox Judaism, Islam and almost all of the Holy Land's Christian churches tend to adamantly oppose homosexuality, so be circumspect in religious neighbourhoods.

LGBTIQ+ Tel Aviv

Tel Aviv has a reputation as one of the world's great destinations for LGBTIQ+ travellers. In June it plays host to the week-long **Tel Aviv Pride**, the region's biggest and most flamboyant gay and lesbian festival. Rainbow flags can be found in cafes and on beaches and the city's hotels are almost all LGBTIQ+ friendly.

LGBTIQ+-focused venues include the hip gay bar Shpagat (p143) and the male-only, hook-up bar-club **Apolo** (☎03-774-1106; www.apolo.co.il; 46 Allenby St; ☼10pm-4am). To keep updated on the latest happenings, check Atraf (www.atraf.com), which has a smartphone app, or the comprehensive Gay Tel Aviv Guide (www.gaytelavivguide.com).

Beachgoers might also want to visit Hilton Beach (p175), Tel Aviv's unofficial gay beach. Check events and club nights (many held at the HaOman 17 venue on Arbarbanel St) when planning your trip at www.gaytelavivguide.com.

The **Tel Aviv LGBTQ Community Centre** (☎03-525-2896; www.lgbtqcenter.org.il; 22 Tchernikhovsky St; ☼10am-10pm Sun-Thu) near Gan Meir Park hosts gay- and lesbian-themed events, lectures, sports groups and potluck picnics.

Tel Aviv Pride

With Tel Aviv's designation as the Middle East's LGBTIQ+ capital, it's no wonder that droves descend upon the city for its annual **Pride festival** (www.

HAFAKOT/SHUTTERSTOCK ©

facebook.com/tlvpride; ⏱ Jun). The week-long celebration welcomes some 250,000 revellers from across the spectrum – gay and straight, young and old, locals and tourists from far and wide. Taking place in the second week of June, International Gay Pride Month, the crown event is a parade that starts at Gan Meir Park and culminates at Charles Clore Garden for a beach party. Other events include film screenings, fitness demonstrations, picnics and fashion shows.

LGBTIQ+ Jerusalem

Videopub (p88) is a gay bar with a tiny dance floor. Email the **Jerusalem Open House for Pride & Tolerance** (☎ 02-625-3191; www.joh.org.il; 1st fl, 2 HaSoreg St; 🚋 City Hall) ahead of time to learn about community events, some of which are English-speaker friendly. In late July or early August, the LGBTIQ+ community takes to the streets in the **Jerusalem March for Pride & Tolerance**. More a human rights demonstration than a carnival, the march urges tolerance of the LGBTIQ+ community and remembers those who were killed and injured in the 2009 Bar-Noar shootings (a targeted attack on the gay community), as well as Shira Banki, who was stabbed to death by an ultra-Orthodox man at the parade in 2015.

For Kids

Travelling with children is generally a breeze: the food's varied and tasty, the distances are short and there are child-friendly activities at every turn. Israeli society is very family-oriented and children are welcome pretty much everywhere.

CHAMELEONSEYE/SHUTTERSTOCK ©

Jerusalem

While Jerusalem's religious and archaeological sights leave adult visitors awed, young children tend not to agree. Ruins and archaeological parks are exhausting for small feet, queues are boring, and hot weather can be a struggle. Luckily, there are many child-friendly sights to mix into a family itinerary.

Tel Aviv

Despite its party reputation, Tel Aviv is as family-friendly as cities get. A baby boom in recent years has seen more families with children living in the city, and thanks to its beaches, parks and tree-lined avenues, TLV is now a top destination for kids.

Best For Kids

Tisch Zoological Gardens (www.jerusalemzoo. org) Let the kids loose in the Biblical Zoo, a 25-hectare park in the southwest of the city. The biblical theme begins at the 'Noah's Ark' visitors centre, continuing with enclosures holding animals mentioned in the Bible, including lions, bears and crocodiles. Other parts of the zoo have worldwide wildlife, from penguins to grey kangaroos.

Gottesman Aquarium (www.israel-aquarium.org.il) This aquarium focuses on regional aquatic life, primarily from the Mediterranean and Red Seas. Kids of all ages will ooh and aah walking through the tunnel underneath one-and-a-half-million litres of undersea habitat and the sting ray feeding pool.

Safari Ramat Gan (www.safari.co.il) Offering a fascinating glimpse of fantastic beasts, this is close as you'll get to the Serengeti plains in Israel. It's both a drive-through safari and a large zoo – the safari section includes rhinos, hippos, zebras and flamingos; the zoo has elephants, giraffes, monkeys, kangaroos and more, plus a petting farm, workshops for children, cafes and picnic areas.

Under the Radar

Jerusalem's history and sacred sights and Tel Aviv's beaches and bars help define the identity of these two contrasting cities, but there are lesser known places to explore that reveal other sides of each.

YURI REDJEBOV/SHUTTERSTOCK ©

Tel Aviv's Architectural Heritage

Central Tel Aviv has more 1930s Bauhaus-style buildings than any other city in the world, so the area known as the 'White City' (roughly the city centre and south city centre) was declared a Unesco World Heritage Site in 2003.

Today, many of these buildings are in a state of disrepair (the heat and desert winds are particularly tough on the concrete), but several hundred have been renovated and each year more are being restored to their former glory. The Bauhaus Centre (p125) offers self-guided and guided walking tours of the area's streets.

Hiking Jerusalem's Forests

Locals looking for fresh air and relative solitude head to the city's nearby forests. The Ramot B area in northern Jerusalem has trails with nice views. You'll see others on weekends, but likely have the place to yourself during the week. Park at Gan Hakipod (a small forested park) and walk away from the kids' play area towards the ridge and you'll find several trail heads into the 'wilderness'. Jackals, Gazella Gazella (the local gazelle species) and rare species of cat are sometimes seen.

To the south is the more remote Ramot forest, while to the southwest is the Beit Guvrin area where you can see ruins, caves and other historical sights on walks; one recommended trail takes you to the top of a hill covered in wildflowers in kibbutz Netiv HaLamed, just off Hwy 375.

Art

The diverse people who call these cities home – from Arab to Druze to Mizrahi and Ashkenazi Jews – has always found its expression in the arts. Jerusalem boasts the impressive Israel Museum, which contains nearly half a million items in its collection; Tel Aviv is a wellspring of innovative galleries and phenomenal street art.

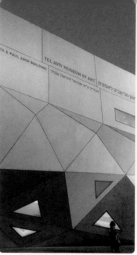

PHOTOGRAPHER: HAFAKOT/SHUTTERSTOCK ©
ARCHITECT: PRESTON SCOTT COHEN

Tel Aviv's Art Scene

Modern, vibrant and cosmopolitan, Tel Aviv is characterised by an enterprising creative landscape. From the world-class Tel Aviv Museum of Art, which houses works by international greats, to the secluded street-art alleys and avant-garde galleries scattered around bohemian Florentin, inspiration comes in myriad mediums. And it doesn't end with the visual arts – there's plenty of performance, too. Enjoy the rich theatre scene, live music ranging from beachside buskers to big-name international acts, and plenty of classical music, opera and ballet for high-culture cats.

Jerusalem's Israel Museum

The museum collection contains nearly half a million items: illuminated religious writings, Jewish traditional dress from around the world and globe-spanning art, including a world-class collection of European masterworks from the 15th to the 21st centuries.

Best Places to Appreciate Art

Israel Museum Fine arts, archaeology and Jewish architecture in a sprawling space. (p175)

Tel Aviv Museum of Art World-class collection of modern art, design and architecture. (p112)

Museum on the Seam Exhibitions that literally and figuratively straddle the line between East and West Jerusalem. (p66)

Tours

ALEXANDER SPATARI/GETTY IMAGES ©

The tourism offices of both Tel Aviv and Jaffa offer many free walking tours. If you're an Old City first-timer, letting someone else show you around is a great way to tackle the top sights in an efficient way; the rest of Jerusalem is easier to navigate at your own pace.

Touring Jerusalem's Old City

The municipality's website (www. itraveljerusalem. com/trs/old-city-self-guided-audio-tours) offers free maps and apps for 15 self-guided audio walking tours of the Old City. Tours are in English, Russian and Hebrew.

Tour guides offering their services outside the Jaffa Gate are often unlicensed; if you need a guide, ask at the tourist office (p174)

or opt for a reputable operator such as Sandemans (p176) or **Green Olive Tours** (☑ 03-721-9540; www. greenolivetours.com).

Jerusalem's Best Individual Guides

Yehuda Kaplan (☑ 054-835-3369; ykaplan29@ gmail.com) Biblical archaeologist and curator at the Bible Lands Museum, Yehuda knows his stuff, but he's also engaging, enthusiastic and accommodating. He requires one week notice and charges by the hour; cost depends on number of people in group.

James Elgrod (☑ 052-640 6507; jameselgrod@ gmail.com) Passionate about the city's archaeology and history, James specialty is the City of David and Old City.

Aryeh Herrmann (☑ 052-284-4048; asia caravan@gmail.com; per day US$350, up to 7 people with van US$650) Haifa native who knows Jerusalem and the region well. Speaks Hebrew, English and Thai.

Yoelish Kraus (☑ 052-636-1676) A member of the ultra-Orthodox community, Yoelish is highly recommended for walking tours of Mea She'arim.

Four Perfect Days

Day 1 – Jerusalem

SALAJEAN/SHUTTERSTOCK ©

Start day one in Jerusalem at the **Temple Mount/Al Haram Ash Sharif** (p34; there are two limited access periods per day for non-Muslims), where its **Dome of the Rock** (p35; pictured) and **Al Aqsa Mosque** (p36) make this the third holiest site for the world's Muslims.

Meander to the majestic **Church of the Holy Sepulchre** (p38), where it's said Jesus was crucified and buried, and take in the scene, architecturally, historically and religiously. Wander the nearby souq and alleyways of the Christian and Muslim quarters at your leisure.

Day 2 – Jerusalem

Begin day two in Jerusalem early at the world-renowned **Israel Museum** (p92), where you need a good half day to do it justice. Check out the Dead Sea Scrolls, the reconstructed synagogues and fine-art collection.

Approach the **Western Wall** (p42; prebook for the Western Wall Tunnels tour), Judaism's holiest prayer site, and after taking in the fascinating scene, lose the afternoon in labyrinthine Jewish Quarter alleys, pausing for panoramic views from **Hurva Synagogue** (p50; pictured), and haggling in the Muslim Quarter's souqs.

Day 3 – Tel Aviv

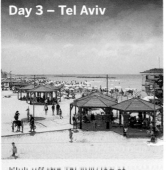

Kick off the Tel Aviv leg of your trip by basking in the sun at **Frishman Beach** (p157; pictured) or **Bograshov Beach** (p157), where you can get a glimpse of the country's favourite seaside pastime, *matkot* (paddle ball).

If you can peel yourself from the sand, spend the afternoon taking in the extensive collection at the **Tel Aviv Museum of Art** (p112). End the day at **Sarona** (p124) market, just south of the museum, where you can wander the outdoor shops before dinner.

Day 4 – Tel Aviv

Kick off your final day with a stroll through **Carmel Market** (p130), sipping a fresh pomegranate juice as you make your way around the stalls. Then head down Allenby St to the Great Synagogue for lunch with the locals at **Port Sa'id** (p138)

Walk off lunch with a stroll around **Rothschild Blvd** (p126). Stop in to the **Independence Hall** (p137; pictured), take in the beautiful Bauhaus architecture and browse a book from one of the pop-up libraries.

Need to Know

For detailed information, see Survival Guide (p169)

Currency
New Israeli Shekel
(NIS)

Language
Hebrew, Arabic,
English, Yiddish

Visas
Israel grants on-
arrival visas to most
nationalities.

Money
ATMs are found across
both cities, including in
Jerusalem's Old City.
Credit cards are widely
accepted.

Time
Israel Standard Time
(November to March;
GMT/UTC plus two
hours); Israel Summer
Time (April to October;
GMT/UTC plus three
hours)

Phones
Smartphones are
ubiquitous and it's
easy to purchase a
local prepaid SIM
card. Whatsapp is the
preferred method of
communicating.

Daily Budget

Budget: Less than 500NIS
Dorm bed: 95NIS
Double bed in a budget hotel: 450NIS
Falafel or hummus: 20NIS
Bus ticket: 6.90NIS

Midrange: 500–1500NIS
Double room in a hotel: 450–750NIS
Brunch in a cafe: 60–80NIS
Admission to museum: 50NIS
Taxi ride: 45NIS

Top end: More than 1500NIS
Double room in a boutique hotel: 1000–2500NIS
Lunch and dinner in a restaurant: 150–300NIS
Private walking tour: 300–400NIS
Hire car: 125NIS

Advance Planning

Three months before Search the calendar for
events and festivals, as well as major holidays
like Ramadan and Yom Kippur that might alter
plans.

One month before Schedule guided tours
of the Old City and make accommodation
arrangements.

One week before Make reservations for concerts, shows and any restaurants that call for
them. Order a Jerusalem City Pass online.

Arriving in Jerusalem

✈ Ben Gurion International Airport

To Jerusalem: taxi (268NIS), sherut (shared taxi; 64NIS) and bus 485 (16NIS or the Jerusalem City Pass); to Tel Aviv: train (every 30 minutes, 14NIS) or taxi (160NIS).

🚍 Allenby Crossing/ King Hussein Bridge

From Jordan; sherut to Jerusalem (40NIS). At least 30 minutes travel time, plus extra for visa and security checks where lines can be long

✈ At the Airport

Ben Gurion International Airport (www.iaa.gov.il) has notoriously thorough security. Arrive at least three hours before your flight and be prepared for detailed questions from security officials.

Getting Around

Jerusalem's Old City and downtown are walkable and the rest of its neighbourhoods are well connected by buses and a light-rail system.

It's easy to walk and bike around Tel Aviv, and a great network of buses makes getting around a breeze. Public transport doesn't run from Friday afternoon to Saturday evening during Shabbat.

Sarona (p124)

Jerusalem Neighbourhoods

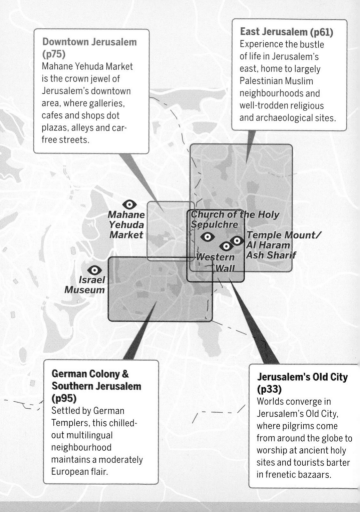

Downtown Jerusalem (p75)
Mahane Yehuda Market is the crown jewel of Jerusalem's downtown area, where galleries, cafes and shops dot plazas, alleys and car-free streets.

East Jerusalem (p61)
Experience the bustle of life in Jerusalem's east, home to largely Palestinian Muslim neighbourhoods and well-trodden religious and archaeological sites.

German Colony & Southern Jerusalem (p95)
Settled by German Templers, this chilled-out multilingual neighbourhood maintains a moderately European flair.

Jerusalem's Old City (p33)
Worlds converge in Jerusalem's Old City, where pilgrims come from around the globe to worship at ancient holy sites and tourists barter in frenetic bazaars.

◉ *Mahane Yehuda Market*

◉ *Church of the Holy Sepulchre*

◉ *Temple Mount/ Al Haram Ash Sharif*

◉ *Western Wall*

◉ *Israel Museum*

Explore Jerusalem

Destroyed and rebuilt over thousands of years, Jerusalem's magnetism endures. With interlacing histories, clashing cultures and constant reinvention, it's an intense, multisensory experience – and a spiritual lightning rod, sacred and affirming to Jews, Muslims and Christians. Wide-eyed with awe, pilgrims flood into the walled city to worship at locations linked to the very foundations of their faith.

Explore ⊕

Jerusalem's Old City

Busy roads roar around the Old City, but within its walls, life continues in the ways it has for centuries. Mornings crackle with energy as pilgrims from around the globe worship at holy sites. Tourists wander its Muslim, Jewish, Christian and Armenian quarters, bargaining in the markets until the late afternoon. This is when the Old City is at its loveliest.

The Old City's icons include the Temple Mount/ Al Haram Ash Sharif (p34), where the Dome of the Rock and Al Aqsa Mosque make it the third holiest site for the world's Muslims; the majestic Church of the Holy Sepulchre (p38), where it is believed Jesus was crucified, buried and then resurrected; and the Western Wall (p42), Judaism's holiest prayer site. For a comprehensive and insightful introduction to the Old City, head to Jaffa Gate (p50) for the 11am Sandemans free walking tour, which covers these major holy sites and more throughout the Jewish, Muslim, Christian and Armenian quarters.

Getting There & Around

There are four major entry points to Jerusalem's Old City: Jaffa Gate (p50), Damascus Gate (p51), Dung Gate (p48) and Lions' Gate (p48). The light rail stops at City Hall (from where it's a short walk to Jaffa or New gates) and Damascus gates.

🚌 Buses 1 and 3 from the Central Station arrive near Dung Gate and the Western Wall.

🚌 A free shuttle goes from the First Station complex in the German Colony to Dung Gate with stops in the Old City.

Jerusalem's Old City Map on p46

Jaffa Gate (p50) ALON ADIKA/SHUTTERSTOCK ©

Top Experience 📷

Visit Jerusalem's holiest site: Temple Mount/Al Haram Ash Sharif

Both the most contentious and holiest site in Jerusalem, the role of Temple Mount/Al Haram Ash Sharif in religious and political history is momentous. The Dome of the Rock, the city's most distinctive landmark with its gold top shimmering above a turquoise-hued octagonal base, is breathtaking. Don't miss the chance to see it and the entire Temple Mount/Al Haram Ash Sharif up close.

◉ MAP P46, E3

admission free

🕑 7.30-11am & 1.30-2.30pm Sun-Thu Apr-Sep, 7.30-10am & 12.30-1.30pm Sun-Thu Oct-Mar

The Layout

Temple Mount/Al Haram Ash Sharif is located on a hill in the southeastern corner of the Old City with the Kidron Valley falling away to the east on the other side of the Old City and the compound's walls. The 35-acre area is largely flat and paved, pockmarked with palm and cypress trees and fringed with attractive Mamluk buildings. The Dome of the Rock is positioned roughly at its centre and the Al Aqsa Mosque at the southern edge. The Western Wall marks the southern boundary. Walking around this storied, spacious site is a true contrast to the noise and congestion of the surrounding narrow alleyways. Today the compound is the biggest public space in East Jerusalem, so along with praying, Palestinian children come to play football and adults come to relax.

Dome of the Rock

The **Dome of the Rock** (Qubbat Al Sakhra), one of the most photographed buildings on the planet, was constructed between 688 and 691 CE under the patronage of the Umayyad caliph Abd Al Malik who wanted to instil a sense of pride in the local Muslim population, keep them loyal to Islam and make a statement to Jews and Christians.

The rotunda of the Church of the Holy Sepulchre was used by Malik's Byzantine architects as a model; however, unlike the dark medieval interiors of churches, their mosque was covered inside and out with a bright confection of mosaics and scrolled verses from the Quran, while the crowning dome was covered in solid gold that shone as a beacon for Islam.

A plaque was laid inside honouring Malik and giving the date of construction. Two hundred years later, the Abbasid caliph Al Mamun altered it to claim credit for himself, neglecting to amend the original date. The Crusaders briefly repurposed it as a church, but it became

★ **Top Tips**

o Dress modestly: both men and women should cover their legs, shoulders, elbows and backs. Visitors deemed by caretakers to be insufficiently clothed will be given a shawl to wear sarong-style.

o Bag searches at the entrance range from thorough to non-existent. Non-Islamic religious objects and texts are prohibited; don't wear religious symbols.

o Non-Muslims are not permitted to enter the Al Aqsa Mosque or the Dome of the Rock; trying to do so is both disrespectful and unwise.

✖ **Take a Break**

There is nowhere to eat or drink on site, so you'll need to leave the complex to fuel up.

Abu Shukri (p53), beloved by locals and tourists alike, serves bowls of rich, smooth hummus with crunchy veg, pita and falafel on the side.

an Islamic shrine again in the 12th century under Saladin. In 1545, Suleiman the Magnificent ordered that the much-weathered exterior mosaics be removed and replaced with tiles. These were again replaced during a major restoration in the 20th century. The original gold dome also disappeared long ago, and the dome you see today is covered with 5000 gold plates donated by the late King Hussein of Jordan. The 80kg of gold cost the king US$8.2 million – he sold one of his homes in London to pay for it.

Inside (non-Muslims are prohibited from entering), lying centrally under the 20m-high dome and ringed by a wooden fence, is the rock from which it is said Muhammad began his *miraj* (ascension to heaven). According to the Quran,

Muhammad pushed the stone down with his foot, leaving a footprint on the rock (supposedly still visible in one corner). Jewish tradition also has it that this marks the centre of the world and where Abraham prepared to sacrifice his son.

Steps below the rock lead to a cave known as the **Well of Souls**, where according to medieval legends the voices of the dead are said to be heard falling into the river of paradise and on to eternity. The *mihrab* (niche indicating the direction of Mecca) in the sanctuary is said to be the the oldest in the Islamic world.

Al Aqsa Mosque

Al Aqsa, which can accommodate up to 5000 worshippers, means 'farthest mosque' in reference to the

Sabil of Qaitbay

journey Muhammad is believed to have made on his way to heaven to receive instructions from Allah. The mosque is off-limits to non-Muslims, who can admire it from the outside.

Originally built by order of the Umayyad caliph Al Walid (r 705–15 CE), Al Aqsa stands on what the Crusaders thought to be the site of the First Temple and what others believe was a marketplace on the edge of the Temple. Some Christians revere it as the location where Jesus turned over the tables and drove out the moneychangers (Matthew 21:13).

Rebuilt at least twice after earthquakes razed it, the mosque was converted into the residence of the kings of Jerusalem after the Crusaders took the city in 1099 CE. On the death of Baldwin II in 1131, the building was handed over to a decade-old order of soldier-monks, whose members soon began referring to themselves as the Templars after their new headquarters. The order added a number of extensions, including the still remaining refectory along the southern wall of the enclosure. The other Crusader structures were demolished by Saladin (Salah Ad Din; 1137–93), the first of the Sunni Ayyubid dynasty, who added an intricately carved *mihrab* (prayer niche indicating the direction of Mecca) to the mosque.

Tragic events have repeatedly struck the mosque during the last century. King Abdullah of Jordan (1882–1951) was assassinated while attending Friday prayers here. In 1969, an arson attack by an Australian visitor irreparably damaged priceless religious objects. In 2017, Israeli metal detectors were temporarily installed at entrances to Al Aqsa, as a response to the shooting of two Israeli police officers; this prompted bloody clashes and several deaths.

Architectural Features

Other significant structures to take note of include the Mamluk-era arched columns above the stairways ascending from the lower plaza to the Dome of the Rock; these are referred to as the **Scales of Souls** since Muslims believe it's here that scales will be hung from the columns to weigh the souls of the dead.

Directly in front of the Dome of the Rock's eastern side is the **Dome of the Chain**, which some believe was built as a model for the larger structure. The **Al Kas Fountain**, located between Al Aqsa Mosque and the Dome of the Rock, is used for ritual washing before prayers. On the western esplanade is the **Sabil of Qaitbay**, a 13m high structure built by Egyptians in 1482 as a charitable act to please Allah.

Make a point of departing via the **Bab Al Qattanin** (Gate of Cotton Merchants), the most imposing of the gates which leads into the Mamluk-era arcaded market of the Cotton Merchants (Souq Al Qattanin).

Top Experience 📷

See five stations of the cross at Church of the Holy Sepulchre

Built on what Helena, Emperor Constantine's mother, believed to be the site of Jesus's crucifixion and burial, the Church of the Holy Sepulchre is the holiest place in the world for many Christians. In darkened chambers infused with incredible spirituality, a variety of Christian denominations keep alive some of the oldest traditions of their faith.

⊙ MAP P46, C4

☎ 02-626-7000

Christian Quarter

🕑 5am-9pm Easter-Sep, to 8pm Sun, 4am-7pm Oct-Easter

Architecture

Don't expect an orderly, simple layout. What you see today is a palimpsest of architectural styles, a mishmash of renovations and additions made over centuries. Besides the clearly defined final five Stations of the Cross, there's a dizzying array of other chapels, tombs and historic sites spread throughout the various parts and levels of the property.

The earliest structure was built in 326 CE after Helena, while on pilgrimage in the Holy City, determined that Hadrian's pagan temple to Venus (built in 135 CE) had been built to thwart early Christians from worshipping here, the site of Cavalry (Latin for 'place of skull', or 'Golgotha' in Aramaic). The emperor agreed to demolish the temple, excavate the tomb of Christ and build a church to house it. From the 4th century, shrines and churches were built, occasionally destroyed by invading armies, including by the mad Caliph Hakim in 1099, and rebuilt on the site.

Restoration began once again in 1010 but moved slowly because money was tight. Two decades later, the Byzantine Imperial Treasury provided a subsidy, though not enough for a complete reconstruction. A large part was abandoned, but an upper gallery in the rotunda and an apse on its eastern side were added. This was the church that the Crusaders entered on 15 July 1099 as the new rulers of Jerusalem. Of course, like occupiers before them, they made significant alterations.

A fire in 1808 and an earthquake in 1927 caused extensive damage; however, disagreements among the Catholic, Greek Orthodox, Armenian Orthodox, Syrian, Coptic and Ethiopian factions who share ownership of the church meant it wasn't until 1959 that a major repair program was agreed upon. The most recent renovations were completed in 2017, when the tomb enjoyed a US$4-million injection of funding to stabilise the shrine – but not before decades of discussions.

★ Top Tips

o Dress modestly – guards are sometimes strict and refuse entry to those with bare legs, shoulders or backs.

o Expect crowds and noise. Get there as early as possible for more quiet reverie.

o On the Friday before Easter Sunday, thousands of pilgrims walk the Procession of the Way of the Cross on Via Dolorosa, and at night, the candlelit Funeral Procession heads to the Church of the Holy Sepulchre.

✕ Take a Break

Just a short walk away, Lina Restaurant (p53) serves some of the Old City's best hummus and falafel.

Stations of the Cross

The final five stations of the Via Dolorosa (p44), the route it's believed Jesus walked on his way to the crucifixion, are located within the church, and casually dressed visitors shuffle reverently through candlelit corridors redolent with incense, while resplendently garbed clergy oversee the parade. The only access is from the southern side of the church and through the left opening of the double doorway.

To reach the first of the church's stations, head up the steep stairway immediately to the right of the entrance. You're ascending the hill of the Calvary, which was outside the city at the time. On the right is the **10th Station of the Cross** in the small Chapel of the Franks; it is believed that Jesus was stripped of his garments here. Behind the wall of the 10th Station is the **11th Station**, the very literally named Catholic Chapel of the Nailing to the Cross, where Jesus is believed to have been pinned to the cross. Check out the 12th-century ceiling mosaic here, the only surviving one from the Crusader era. The site of Jesus's death, the Rock of Calvary, is the gaudily ornate and Gothic **12th Station**, known as the Chapel of Crucifixion, which is administered by the Greek Orthodox Church; an altar built with a hole in it allows pilgrims to touch the limestone rock. Between these two is the **13th Station**, the Our Lady of Sorrows Altar, where Jesus's body is said to have been taken down from the cross.

Back down the stairs, it's impossible to miss the rotunda surrounded

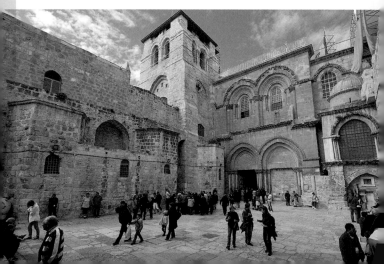

by massive pillars housing the **14th Station**, the multichambered **Tomb of the Holy Sepulchre**, where it's said Jesus was buried and subsequently rose from the dead. Technically, it's referred to as an edicule, a shrine shaped like a monument, and it's flanked by huge candles. Cleared of soot and debris in the latest round of restoration work, high-tech architectural spectrometry also revealed that it contains the remains of several previous structures. Watch your head when ducking through the low doorway to the inner chamber, which is lined with marble and hung with religious pictures and icons.

Other Chapels & Sights

Directly in front of the entrance to the Church of the Holy Sepulchre is the **Stone of Anointing**, a slab of rock overhung with a row of lamps and flanked by large candelabra, usually lined with emotional visitors deep in prayer. Historians have established, however, that it is not the actual stone where Jesus was laid before burial.

Bolstering the argument that the site of the Church of the Holy Sepulchre was once outside the city proper are several 1st-century **Jewish tombs** found through a low entrance behind the Tomb of the Holy Sepulchre.

The Franciscan **Chapel of Apparition** was built on the site where it's said Jesus appeared to his mother after his resurrection. On the right side is the 'column of flagellation', the very column on which it's claimed Jesus was flogged. A series of modern bronze statues depicting all of the Stations of the Cross are displayed on a ledge on the far side of the chapel.

You can see the rock of Calvary (or hill) in glass-screened **Chapel of Adam**, directly below the Chapel of Crucifixion. Some traditions claim the biblical Adam was buried here and that the crack visible in the rock resulted from an earthquake that occurred at the moment Jesus died.

Another chapel called the **Prison of Christ** is where it's said Jesus was held before his crucifixion. The **Chapel of St Longinus** is dedicated to the Roman soldier said to have speared Jesus and soon after repented and accepted Jesus' divinity.

The subterranean Armenian **Chapel of St Helena** (pictured on p38) and Franciscan **Chapel of the Finding of the Cross** are dedicated to Helena, emperor Constantine's mother, who is said found the actual cross of the crucifixion. The latter is carved out of rock, in an area that's thought to have once been a cistern.

Top Experience 📷

Tour the tunnels under the Western Wall

For centuries, Jews have come to the 2000-year-old western retaining wall of the Temple Mount to pray and to mourn the destruction of the First and Second Temples. The Western Wall's enormous stones, worn smooth by countless caresses, have an almost magnetic power, drawing close the hands and foreheads of the faithful, who come in search of a deep, direct connection with God.

◉ MAP P46, E4

www.thekotel.org

Jewish Quarter

🕓 24hr

Prayer

The area immediately in front of the Wall operates as a great open-air synagogue, exerting a pull discernible even to nonreligious visitors. It's divided into two areas: a small southern section for women and a much larger northern section for men. Here, black-garbed ultra-Orthodox men rock on their heels, bobbing their heads in prayer, occasionally breaking to press themselves against the Wall and kiss the stones. Women face greater challenges to freely worship at the Wall, whose Orthodox custodians remain deeply uncomfortable with female voices reciting here. The Kotel Agreement is meant to resolve the tensions.

Wads of paper are stuffed into the cracks between the stones; some believe that prayers and petitions inserted between the stones have a greater chance of being answered. These are never thrown away – periodically, the attendants will gather the notes that have fallen on the ground, and they are interred with the next person buried on the Mount of Olives.

Tunnels

It's no surprise that the subterranean layers of this area have become as politically and religiously fraught as the world above. Archaeologists have been excavating and exploring the **Western Wall tunnels** (☏02-627-1333; www.thekotel.org; Jewish Quarter; adult/student & child 35/19NIS; ⏱by tour only 7am-5pm) for decades, and continue to do so.

Shuffling through the reinforced tunnels, you can easily forget their age. Look up and see the remains of arches for a bridge walkway that once ran between Jaffa Gate and Temple Mount.

The **Behind the Scenes** (adult/child 40/25NIS; reservations required) tour takes visitors to dig sites. Locations change weekly and aren't settled until the day of the tour.

★ Top Tips

o Modest dress is recommended for all visitors (if in doubt, cover from shoulders to knees). Men should grab one of the free kippa (skullcap worn by observant Jewish men) in a basket before approaching the wall.

o There's always a crowd at sunset on Friday for Shabbat. Bar mitzvahs are usually held on Shabbat or on Monday and Thursday mornings, this is a great times to visit, as the area is alive with families singing and dancing.

o Photography is prohibited on Shabbat, as is writing in the entire plaza – keep this in mind if you want to leave a prayer in the Wall.

✖ Take a Break

Hurva Sq has more than half a dozen fast food options, including **BBQ Meat & Grill** (☏02-627-7788; 1 Hamekubalin St, Jewish Quarter; mains 25-72NIS; ⏱11am-10pm Sun-Thu, to 3pm Fri), as well as a good ice cream and smoothie place.

Walking Tour 🥾

Via Dolorosa

The Via Dolorosa (Way of the Sorrows; Muslim Quarter) is the route that Jesus is believed to have taken as he carried his cross to Calvary. Its history goes back to the days of the earliest Byzantine pilgrims, who trod the path from Gethsemane to Calvary on Holy Thursday.

Walk Facts

Start Via Dolorosa, 1st Station

End Church of the Holy Sepulchre

Length 600m; one to 1½ hours

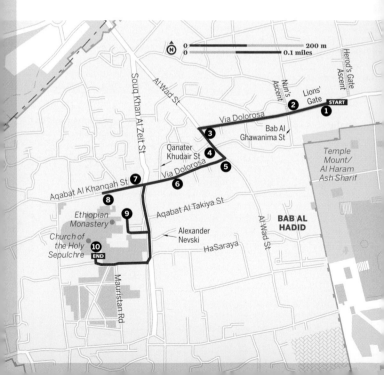

❶ 1st Station

The **1st Station**, where Pontius Pilate is said to have condemned Jesus, is inside the Al Omariyeh school; the entrance is the brown door at the top of the ramp.

❷ 2nd Station

The **2nd Station** (⏱multimedia show 8am-5pm), where it's believed Jesus received the cross, is across the street in the Franciscan Church of the Condemnation.

❸ 3rd Station

Continue down to Al Wad St and turn left to the **3rd Station**, where it's believed Jesus fell for the first time. It's in the chapel to the left of the Armenian Catholic Patriarchate Hospice.

❹ 4th Station

The **4th Station**, an area of stones at the entrance to the chapel, marks where Jesus is said to have faced his mother in the crowd of onlookers.

❺ 5th Station

As Al Wad St continues towards the south, the Via Dolorosa breaks off to the west; the **5th Station**, where it's believed the Romans ordered Simon the Cyrene to help Jesus carry the cross, is on the corner.

❻ 6th Station

Further along the street, the **6th Station** is marked by a brown wooden door on the left. This is where Veronica is believed to have wiped Jesus's face.

❼ 7th Station

Continue to Souq Khan Al Zeit St. The **7th Station**, where it's believed Jesus fell for the second time, is a small chapel marked by signs on the souq's wall.

❽ 8th Station

Cross Souq Khan Al Zeit St to Aqabat Al Khanqah St. In the left wall is the cross marking the **8th Station**, where it's said Jesus told some women to cry for themselves and their children, not for him.

❾ 9th Station

Backtrack to Souq Khan Al Zeit St and turn right. Take the stairway on your right and follow the path to the Coptic church. The remains of a column in its door mark the **9th Station**, where it is believed Jesus fell for the third time.

❿ The Remaining Five Stations

Head through the Ethiopian Monastery to reach the **Church of the Holy Sepulchre** (p38), which houses the remaining stations..

Temple Mount/Al Haram
Ash Sharif

Al Kas
Fountain

**Western
Wall**

Western

St Anne's
Church **14**

Burj Laqlaq

Simtat
Salahiya

Antonia

Al Ghazali Sq

Sheikh
Hassan

Lions' Gate

Bab Hutta
St

Sha'ar HaPrakhim

Via Dolorosa

Little
Western
Wall

5 Western
Wall

26

HaTsari'akh

Herod's Gate
Ascent

6

Bab Al
Ghawanima **19**

Tariq Bab
An Nazir St

HaTsari'akh Ha'Adom

Nun's
Ascent

Terra Sancta
Museum

Al Wad St

Tariq Bab
El Hadid St

Bab El Silsila St

El Mawlawiya

**MUSLIM
QUARTER**

27

Via Dolorosa

Aqabat Al
Khalidiyya

Sa'adiya

Al Wad St

HaSaraya

Zedekiah's Cave

21

Aqabat Al Takiya St

Ha-Kari

7

HaShtikhim

Mauristan Rd

Lutheran
Church of
the Redeemer

13

25

Souq Khan Al Zeit St

29 **30 22**

Aqabat Al Khanqah St

**Church of the
Holy Sepulchre**

Dabbaga Rd

17

8

Mauristan

Sultan Suleiman St

HaKnesiyot

El Jabsha

Christian Quarter Rd

**CHRISTIAN
QUARTER**

HaKoptim

31

HaNevi'im St

Damascus
Gate

Misht'ol
HaPninim
Garden

Greek Orthodox
Patriarchate Rd

HaKoptim

St Francis St

Greek Catholic
Patriarchate Rd

HaAyin Het St

Bab El
Jadid Rd

Casa Nova Rd

St Dimitri's
Rd

32 35

HaAkhim St

Les Freres St

Latin
Patriarchate
Rd

23

Khulda HaNevi'a St

Elisha St

Mamilla Ma

Damascus Gate

HaTsanhanim Rd

Bab Al Maghariba

Jerusalem
Archaeological Park
& Davidson Centre 3

Ma'Alot Ir David Rd

Wadi Hilwa St

Ma'aleh Shalom Rd

Misgav Ladach

Tiferet 36
33 Yisae
11   12   6 16
Stone Ha-Kipot
Jewish Quarter R Herodian
Quarter
Museum
Hurva
11 9
Hurva   Batei Mahseh Sq
M'Mark's
St   10 34 4
Habad St   Synagogue Batei
Cardo   Maḥseh St
Or Ha:Chaim St   Maximus
JEWISH
Ararat St   Batei Mahsen St
QUARTER
Ma'alam St

ARMENIAN   Armenian
QUARTER   Orthodox
Patria'chate Rd

P room of
the Last
Supper 15

1
Tower of
David
David's 2
Walk   24

Jaffa Gate 9
Omar Ibn St al Halal St
Arts & Crafts
Lane

Itskhak Kariv Rd

Hativat Zion Rd   Armenian
Catholic
Cemetery   Armenian
Cemetery
Church & 4
Monastery of
the Dormition   Grave of
Oskar
Schindler
18

Hativat Etsyoni St

Hativat Yerushalayim St

Feit St

Eli'el
15 St Yo'els St   Dror Eli'el Rd
Teddy
Kollek
Park

For reviews see

◆ Top Experiences	p34
⊙ Sights	p48
⊗⊘ Eating	p53
⊕⊕ Drinking	p54
✦ Entertainment	p55
⊜ Shopping	p56

0   200 m
0   0.1 miles

N

A B C D E F

Sights

Tower of David
MUSEUM

1 MAP P46, B5

First things first: despite being referred to as the 'Tower of David', the citadel dominating views as you enter Jaffa Gate started life as a palace of Herod the Great. Also used by the Romans and Crusaders, the structure was extensively remodelled by the Mamluks and the Ottomans. Today it's home to the impressive **Museum of the History of Jerusalem**, which tells the city's story in a series of chronologically arranged exhibits starting in the 2nd millennium BCE and finishing in 1948. (Citadel; info 02-626-5333, tour reservations 02-626-5347; www.tod.org.il; Omar Ibn Al Khattab Sq; adult/student/child 40/30/18NIS; 9am-4pm Sat-Thu, to 5pm Jul & Aug, 9am-2pm Fri)

Ramparts Walk
HISTORIC SITE

2 MAP P46, B5

For a rooftop perspective of this ancient city with inspiring views at every step, try this shade-free walk atop the Old City ramparts built by Suleiman the Magnificent around 485 years ago. Two stretches are accessible, from Jaffa Gate (p50) south to **Dung Gate**, and from Jaffa Gate north and west to **Lions' Gate** (St Stephen's Gate; Muslim Quarter), both gruelling in the midday sun. Temple Mount/Al Haram Ash Sharif's ramparts are off-limits. Buy tickets at the tourist office (p174) near Jaffa Gate. (adult/child 18/8NIS; both sections 9am-4pm Sat-Thu Oct-Mar, to 5pm Apr-Sep, southern ramparts 9am-2pm Fri Sep-May, to 8pm Jun-Aug)

Jerusalem Archaeological Park & Davidson Centre
HISTORIC SITE

3 MAP P46, E5

Pore over the remains of streets, columns, gates, walls, plazas and *mikve'ot* (Jewish ritual baths) at this archaeological site near Dung Gate. An audio guide is a helpful accompaniment at the open-air portion of the site, while video presentations (in Hebrew and English) at the visitors centre give an overview of the main excavations in the 1970s and reconstruct the site as it looked 2000 years ago. (02-627-7550; www.rova-yehudi.org.il/sites/archaeological-park-davidson-center; Jewish Quarter; adult/student & child 30/16NIS, guided tour 160NIS, audio guide 5NIS; 8am-5pm Sun-Thu, to 2pm Fri)

Church & Monastery of the Dormition
CHURCH

4 MAP P46, B7

With its round sandstone tower and graceful Romanesque-style arches, the Dormition Church is one of Jerusalem's most recognisable landmarks. The church occupies the site traditionally believed to be where the Virgin Mary died (the word 'dormition' means a peaceful sleep or painless death). The current church and monastery, owned by the German Benedictine order, was consecrated in 1906. Turn left upon entering for the stairs down to the womb like **crypt**, where carved pillars surround a shrine to Mary. Dress modestly. (☎02-565-5330; www.dormitio.net; Mt Zion; admission free; ☉9am-5pm Mon-Sat, from 11.30am Sun)

Little Western Wall RELIGIOUS SITE

5 ◎ MAP P46, E3

Little known and seldom visited by tourists, this small section of the Second Temple–period Temple Mount enclosure (the upper rows of stones are from later periods) attracts religious Jews, men and women, who pray in this quiet alleyway. (Kotel Katan; Sha'ar HaBarzel St, Muslim Quarter)

Terra Sancta Museum MUSEUM

6 ◎ MAP P46, D2

Yet another high-quality archaeology museum in the city, this one run by the Franciscans and showcasing their New Testament–period collection of artefacts, including ossuaries (stone boxes filled with bones of the dead) with Aramaic and Hebrew inscriptions. Visitors follow a path through the ruins of two medieval buildings. Opened in July 2018, it's part of the same compound as the Franciscan Church of the Condemnation and Chapel of the Flagellation, the 2nd Station (p45) of the Via Dolorosa (☎058 550-2736; www. terrasanctamuseum.org; Via Dolorosa,

Tower of David

Muslim Quarter; 15NIS; ⏰9am-6pm Apr-Sep, to 5pm Oct-Mar)

Zedekiah's Cave HISTORIC SITE

7 ◉ MAP P46, C1

A good chunk of the limestone used to build the city above came from this 9000-sq-metre underground cavern. Used on and off from the Second Temple period to the 16th century, it was rediscovered in 1854 by American missionary James Barclay, with the help of his dog. Freemasons, who continue to hold meetings here, believe it was the source of stone used for Solomon's Temple. Others think treasures are waiting to be revealed. It's just north of Damascus Gate. (Solomon's Quarry; 📞02-627-7550; tourism@pamico. il; Sultan Suleiman St; adult/child 18/10NIS; ⏰9am-4pm Sun-Thu, to 5pm May-Sep)

Mauristan HISTORIC SITE

8 ◉ MAP P46, C4

The Mauristan, a Persian word meaning 'hospital' or 'hospice', has a 19th-century fountain at its centre and leads to two souqs (one full of butcher shops) that link to David St. The plaza was an urban market under the Romans. The Crusaders established churches with attached hospices here; one of them, **St John the Baptist** (Christian Quarter; ⏰hours vary), still exists, although its hospice building is long gone. Today, lined by clothing and souvenir shops, it's a

relatively relaxed and roomy place to stroll. (Christian Quarter)

Jaffa Gate GATE

9 ◉ MAP P46, B5

One of the city's six original gates built by order of Suleiman the Magnificent, Jaffa Gate has an imposing entryway that bends at an abrupt right angle as you enter (a design feature to slow down charging enemies). The breach in the wall was made in 1898 to permit German Kaiser Wilhelm II to ride with full pomp into the city (Allenby entered by foot in 1917 to signify how different the British would be); these days taxis and tourists trundle in.

Cardo Maximus HISTORIC SITE

10 ◉ MAP P46, C6

The Cardo was originally a 22m-wide colonnaded avenue flanked by roofed arcades, the main artery of Roman and Byzantine Jerusalem. Following excavations in 1975, a southern swath of the broad avenue, 2.5m below present street level, was reconstructed, while another section has been reshaped into an arcade full of art boutiques. (Jewish Quarter)

Hurva Synagogue SYNAGOGUE

11 ◉ MAP P46, C5

To the local Jewish community, the reconstructed Hurva Synagogue is a symbol of resilience. The earliest synagogue on this spot was wrecked in the early 18th century, and its 19th century successor fell during the 1948 Arab-Israeli War. The broad-domed edifice standing today was dedicated in 2010, and the best reason to visit is to clamber up the tower for peerless views of the Jewish Quarter's rooftops. It also has the world's largest Torah Ark. (Ruin Synagogue; ☏02-626-5900; www.rova-yehudi.org.il; Hurva Sq, Jewish Quarter; adult/student 20/10NIS; ⏰9am-5pm Sun-Thu, to 1pm Fri Oct-Apr, to 7pm Sun-Thu, to 1pm Fri May-Sep)

Hurva Square SQUARE

12 ◉ MAP P46, D5

The beating heart of the Old City's Jewish Quarter, Hurva Sq thrums with life: tourists rustle heritage maps of the city, children scamper around the plaza, and monochrome-clad families sweep to the synagogue. With fast-food restaurants, classy jewellery and Judaica boutiques, and lots of outdoor seating, Hurva Sq is a good place to catch your breath between museums. (Jewish Quarter)

Damascus Gate GATE

13 ◉ MAP P46, C2

The sights and sounds of the Muslim Quarter intensify on the approach to Damascus Gate, on the northern wall of the Old City. The gate's triangular crenellations give it the appearance of a crown; for the best view, walk through the gate to a small stone plaza, surveyed by armed Israeli soldiers, facing Derekh Shchem (Nablus) Rd. (Muslim Quarter)

St Anne's Church CHURCH

14 ◉ MAP P46, F2

The finest example of Crusader architecture in Jerusalem, St Anne's was completed in 1138 on a site thought to have been the home of Joachim and Anne, parents of the Virgin Mary. One of the sunken pools accessed from the rear of the church compound is traditionally thought to be the biblical **Pool of Bethesda** where Jesus is said to have healed a sick man (John 5:1–18). Many groups walking the Via Dolorosa (p44) stop here first. (Sha-ar HaArayot Rd, Muslim Quarter; adult/student & child 10/8NIS; ⏰8am-noon & 2-6pm Apr-Sep, to 5pm Mon-Sat Oct-Mar)

Room of the Last Supper CHRISTIAN SITE

15 ◉ MAP P46, C7

Medieval beliefs about the location of the Last Supper have embedded the Coenaculum (Latin for dining hall) in Christian tradition. Most historians agree that this hall is unlikely to be built on the spot where Jesus ate his final meal. Nonetheless, this elegantly ribvaulted chamber (formerly part of the 4th-century Holy Zion church) usually teems with pilgrims. Retaining the 14th-century Crusader structure that replaced the original church, it was converted to a mosque during the Ottoman period. (Cenacle, Coenaculum; Mt Zion; admission free; ⏰8am-6pm)

Damascus Gate (p51)

Herodian Quarter Museum
ARCHAEOLOGICAL SITE

16  MAP P46, D5

Descend to Jerusalem's ancient bones at this subterranean museum. Among its impressively intact archaeological sites is a 600-sq-m Herodian-era mansion, complete with ritual baths, thought to have belonged to a high priest. Other displays provide a tantalising portal to the past: one mosaic shows evidence of fire damage, thought to date to the conflagration at the First Temple site. It's worth grabbing an audio guide (5NIS). (Wohl Archaeological Museum; ☏072-393-2833; www.rova-yehudi.org.il/sites/the-herodian-quarter; 1 HaKara'im St, Jewish Quarter; adult/concession 20/10NIS; ⏱9am-5pm Sun-Thu, to 1pm Fri)

Lutheran Church of the Redeemer
CHURCH

17  MAP P46, C4

The square bell tower of this Protestant church, the second built in Jerusalem, has ornamented the Old City's skyline since 1898. The Church of the Redeemer was commissioned by Kaiser Wilhelm II and built on the site of an 11th-century sanctuary. It's worth buying a ticket to access the tower for 360-degree views over the Old City – hold your breath: its winding stairs are a squeeze. (☏02-626-6800; Mauristan Rd, Chrisitan Quarter; crypt & tower adult/child 15/7.50NIS; ⏱10am-noon & 2-6pm Mon-Sat)

Grave of Oskar Schindler
MEMORIAL

18 MAP P46, B8

Austrian industrialist Oskar Schindler (1908–74) earned the honorific of Righteous Among the Nations, awarded by Israel to non-Jews who risked their lives to save Jews during the Holocaust. Schindler rescued more than 1200 Jews from the gas chambers by employing them in his factory. His grave is in the Catholic cemetery on Mt Zion. From Zion Gate walk directly ahead, downhill. Once inside the Christian cemetery, descend the steps to the lowest level (Mt Zion; ⏱8am-noon Mon-Sat)

Eating

Abu Shukri
MIDDLE EASTERN $

19 MAP P46, D3

Abu Shukri is so popular that it's spawned imitators around Jerusalem. The standard platter includes a bowl of rich, smooth hummus – topped with chickpeas, tahina (sesame-seed paste), *fuul* (stewed fava beans) or pine nuts – crunchy veg and a basket of pita bread. Be sure to add a side order of falafel (10NIS). Cash only. (📞02-627-1538; 63 Al Wad (Hagai) St, Muslim Quarter; hummus 20NIS; ⏱8am-4.30pm; ✍)

Abu Kamel
MIDDLE EASTERN $$

20 MAP P46, C4

Tucked into a cave-like corner of the Muslim Quarter, just off the Mouristan Market, Abu Kamel serves some of the city's best hummus, topped with pine nuts. Daily specials might include *makloubeh* (roasted vegetables, spices, rice and meat) or *quzi* (peas, carrots, rice with chicken or meat). (📞02-627-6756; Abtimos Market, Muslim Quarter; mains 35NIS; ⏱7am-7pm)

Family Restaurant
MIDDLE EASTERN $$

21 MAP P46, C3

A Middle Eastern grill and hummus restaurant that ticks all the boxes. As the name suggests, you'll see families galore crowding out this canteen-style joint in the Muslim Quarter. Established in 1942, it's clean and consistent, and serves grilled skewers and half-chickens, spreads of hummus, pita and salads, best washed down with mint-infused lemonade. (📞02-628-3435; Souq Khan Al Zeit St, Muslim Quarter; mains from 30NIS; ⏱8am-7pm)

Lina Restaurant
MIDDLE EASTERN $

22 MAP P46, C3

In the running for best Old City hummus and falafel joint, Lina's moreish hummus – usually glistening with olive oil – is among Jerusalem's best. There are two dining rooms on opposite sides of the street, though this unassuming spot is easy to miss. (📞02-627-7230; 42 Aqabat Al Khanqah St, Muslim Quarter; hummus 20NIS; ⏱8am-4.30pm)

Rossini's Restaurant

INTERNATIONAL $$

23 ⊗ MAP P46, B4

Various factors place this rather average steak and pasta place directly in the sights of tourists: it's open on Shabbat, it serves alcohol, and it's steps from Jaffa Gate (p50). Rossini's feels modern and relatively upscale, and the meaty main courses, including *musakhan* (Palestinian-style chicken, onions and sumac on bread) hit the spot after a day of rambling the Old City. (☎02-587-7423; 42 Latin Patriarchate Rd, Christian Quarter; mains 45-130NIS; ☉noon-11pm; ☎; 🚋City Hall)

Christ Church Cafe

CAFE $$

24 ⊗ MAP P46, B5

Decorated with Bible quotes, this cafe near Jaffa Gate nurtures a cosy, collegiate atmosphere and is usually brimming with excitable residents of the adjoining guest-house. Pizza, salads and sandwiches are served until 3.30pm, though the biggest drawcards are perhaps the soft-serve ice cream and the selection of cheesecakes, carrot cake and lemon loaf. A peaceful oasis in the Old City. (☎02-627-7727; Omar Ibn Al Khattab Sq; mains 20-60NIS; ☉9am-8pm Mon-Sat, to 4pm Sun; ☎)

Jaafar Sweets

DESSERTS $

25 ⊗ MAP P46, C2

It's a hypnotic sight, watching pieces of bright-orange, syrup-soaked *kunafeh* (soft cheese topped with shredded pastry) carved from a huge tray. *Kunafeh* is the signature sweet of this well-established Palestinian dessert vendor. Jaafar is also noteworthy for selling well-wrapped trays of baklava and Turkish delight (also unusually, they're labelled with fixed prices); handy for a takeaway. (40-42 Souq Khan Al Zeit St, Muslim Quarter; desserts from 15NIS; ☉8am-7pm Sat-Thu)

Drinking

Musa's Cafe

CAFE

26 ☕ MAP P46, E4

Musa's Cafe is an Old City staple, nestled amid stalls of clothes, sweets and souvenirs in the Cotton Market section of the Muslim Quarter. With seating inside and outside, this simple cafe is a perfect place to reboot with a strong coffee or tea, just like the locals do. (Souq Al Qattanin, Muslim Quarter; ☉7am-7pm)

Viennese Café

CAFE

27 ☕ MAP P46, D2

Baroque music and Sachertorte attempt to carve out a corner of Vienna within the tranquil confines of the Austrian Hospice. Make no mistake: this is a canteen, but with the guilty pleasures of apple strudel, good cups of tea and schnitzel. (Austrian Hospice, 37 Via Dolorosa, Muslim Quarter; ☉10am-10pm; ☎)

Rossini's Restaurant

Versavee CAFE

28 MAP P46, B4

Whether you're sipping mint infused lemonade or a glass of wine, Versavee's courtyard seating and location by Jaffa Gate make it a convenient spot for quick refreshment. It's right next to the Hotel New Imperial and is styled with the same pleasant mix of shabbiness and 19th-century grandeur. (📞02-627-6160; www.versavee.com; Greek Patriarchate Rd; ⏰10am-late; 📶)

Amigo Emil CAFE

29 MAP P46, C3

Arches of Jerusalem stone and the glint of wine racks make this restaurant, housed in a 400-year-old former workshop,

an atmospheric place for a drink, though service is very variable in quality. (📞02-628-8090; 15 Aqabat Al Khanqah St, Christian Quarter; ⏰11am-9.30pm Mon-Sat)

Entertainment

Zedekiah's Cave LIVE MUSIC

This could well be the most unique and atmospheric performance venue in a city with no shortage of them. Top Israeli musicians and bands perform in this underground cave (see 7 Map p46, C1) with candles illuminating the throngs of people. There's also a bar. Check the venue's Facebook page for the irregular schedule. (Solomon's Quarry; www.facebook.com/zedekiyahu caveevents; near Damascus Gate; 75NIS; ⏰performances 9pm Thu)

Zedekiah's Cave (p50)

Shopping

Elia Photo Service   PHOTOGRAPHY

30 🔒 MAP P46, C3

Browse through dramatic historic B&W photos of the Old City and other sights in Jerusalem from before 1967, shot by well-known Armenian photographer Elia Kahvedjian. The shop is run by his grandson. (📞02-628-2074; 14 Al Khanka St, Christian Quarter; 🕙9am-6pm Mon-Sat)

EK Ceramic   CERAMICS

31 🔒 MAP P46, B4

Several generations of the Kouz family have sold high-quality Armenian-style ceramics out of this shopfront. And this will be the last. No offspring will take over from Elie, a friendly, independent man who has bucked trends and sells all of his goods at fixed prices. Pieces don't break or scratch – Elie is happy to prove it. (26 & 28A Christian Quarter St; 🕙10.30am-6.30pm Mon-Fri)

Sandrouni Armenian Art Centre   CERAMICS

32 🔒 MAP P46, A3

After you stroll through New Gate into Jerusalem's Old City, it's hard to resist taking a peek inside the colourful ceramics workshop of Armenian brothers George and Dorin Sandrouni. Since setting up their atelier in 1983, they have been crafting traditional Armenian ceramic designs: pomegranate-shaped ornaments, decorative plates, and tiles patterned with fish, flowers and peace symbols. (☎02-626-3744; www.sandrouni. com; 4 HaAkhim St, Christian Quarter; ⏱9.30am-7pm Mon-Sat)

Heifetz
GIFTS & SOUVENIRS

33 🔒 MAP P46, D5

Traditional Jewish ritual items are given a fresh, contemporary overhaul at Benny Heifetz' studio, where he crafts silver Torah pointers, jaggedly geometric candelabra and a lovely range of jewellery with Jewish themes (such as sparkling Stars of David and chais). (☎02-628 0061; www. bennyheifetz.com; 24 Tiferet Israel Rd, Jewish Quarter; ⏱10am-5pm Sun-Thu, to 2pm Fri)

Moriah
JEWELLERY

34 🔒 MAP P46, C5

Situated in a lovely old house near the Hurva Synagogue (p50), this upmarket shop sells jewellery made with gold, diamonds and fragments of Jerusalem stone excavated during archaeological digs, fashioned into smooth,

teardrop pendants and earrings. (☎02-627-4050; www.moriah-collec tion.com; 7 Beit El St, Jewish Quarter; ⏱10am-6pm Sun-Thu, to 2pm Fri)

Bint Al Balad Workshop & Café
ARTS & CRAFTS

35 🔒 MAP P46, A3

Operated by the Arab Orthodox Society, this craft shop sells embroidered clothing, bags, purses and pillows made by West Bank women working to preserve Palestinian handicraft traditions. Also on offer are Palestinian-style pastries and coffee. (☎02-627-7333, 02-628-1377; HaAkhim St, Christian Quarter; ⏱9am-3pm Mon-Sat; 🚉City Hall)

Moriah Books & Judaica
BOOKS

36 🔒 MAP P46, D5

The Old City's largest Jewish bookstore, plus Judaica and souvenirs, located across from the massive Wohl Torah Centre and just below Hurva Square. (www. moriah.co; 40 Misgav Ladach, Jewish Quarter; ⏱10am-8.30pm Sun-Thu, to 2.30pm Fri)

Walking Tour

Mt Zion

Several important events are said to have occurred at this hill, the highest point in ancient Jerusalem, just south of the Armenian Quarter of the Old City.

Walk Facts

Start Zion Gate

End Church & Monastery of the Dormition

Length 1km; two hours

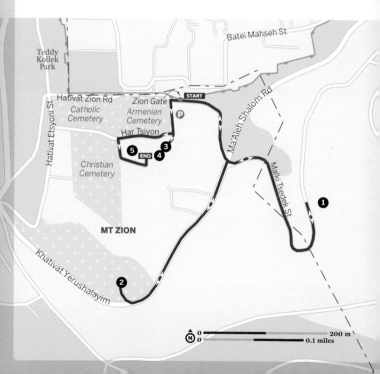

1 Church of St Peter in Gallicantu

Zion Gate makes sense as a starting point; it's easy to find and there's some shade. Almost directly across the street is Malki Tsedek St; follow it for around 100m downhill and you come to the parking lot (on your right and usually filled with loads of tour buses) and the entrance to the **Church of St Peter in Gallicantu** (☎02-673-1739; www.stpeter-gallican tu.org; Mt Zion; adult/child 10/5NIS; ⏰8.30am-5pm Mon-Sat). Built on the foundations of previous Byzantine and Crusader churches, the exterior of this 1930s structure is less impressive than the views of the Palestinian village of Silwan. Inside, there are some unusual stained-glass windows and the exposed foundations and mosaics of earlier churches, including where three Byzantine-era crosses were found.

2 Grave of Oskar Schindler

Retrace your steps back up Malki Tsedek St and turn left on Khativat Yerushalayim St (aka Ma'ale HaShalom St) and follow it down to the Catholic cemetery near the bottom of Mt Zion. Here you'll find the grave of Oskar Schindler (p53), an Austrian industrialist who saved more than 1200 Jewish lives during the Holocaust; it's easy to recognise as it's covered in small stones (a Jewish custom signifying respect).

3 King David's Tomb

Make your way back uphill towards Zion Gate, passing the parking lot again (this time on your left) and into the courtyard of the Franciscan Monastery. Pass an arch and stairway and follow signage to **King David's Tomb** (Mt Zion; admission free; ⏰8am-5pm Sun-Thu, to 1pm Fri), a rather unprepossessing space, for a biblical figure at least. It's to the right of a functioning prayer hall and covered in velvet.

4 Room of the Last Supper

Accessed via the nearby staircase and directly above, in a classic case of Jerusalem's layered history, is the Room of the Last Supper (p51) – at least that's what Christian tradition holds; historical evidence suggests otherwise. The vaulted chamber is usually filled with pilgrims.

5 Church & Monastery of the Dormition

Back down the stairs and to the front of the building, take a short walk down Har Tsiyon St to the entrance of the Romanesque-style Church & Monastery of the Dormition (p48), where it's said the Virgin Mary died. The crypt is down the stairs to the left after entering. Various chapels on the ground floor are dedicated to saints.

Explore ⊕
East Jerusalem

Tourists, embassy workers and some Jewish Israelis mill among East Jerusalem's largely Palestinian Muslim neighbourhoods. Several well-trodden religious and archaeological sites are here, though some visit purely to experience the rhythms of daily life: busy bakeries, markets and the hypnotic sound of the muezzin's call to prayer, louder here than elsewhere in the city.

Begin your visit to East Jerusalem by taking in the politically minded contemporary art at the Museum on the Seam (p66). Only a few blocks away is the thought-provoking Palestinian Heritage Museum (p67). If you have time, stop in to browse the excellent selection of English-language books at the Educational Bookshop (p73). Next, tour the Mount of Olives, the location of momentous biblical events, making time for the cavernous Tomb of the Virgin Mary (p67), the Garden of Gethsemane (p69) and the evocative Church of All Nations (p67) nearby.

Getting There & Around

East Jerusalem is easy to reach via the Damascus Gate after visiting the Old City. The light rail, which has several convenient stops, is the easiest way to get here from West Jerusalem. East Jerusalem's bus routes are privately run; Rav-Kav cards, which can be used on most buses in the Greater Jerusalem area, are not valid for the blue-and-white East Jerusalem buses. Many taxi drivers will refuse to bring you from west to east. Not a problem the other way around.

🚌 The bus station is located on Sultan Suleiman St near Herod's Gate.

East Jerusalem Map on p64

Mount of Olives (p62) ARKA38/SHUTTERSTOCK ©

Walking Tour 🥾

Mount of Olives Walk

As the faithful believe, this is where God will start to redeem the dead when the Messiah returns on Judgment Day. Many Jews choose to be buried here, and to date some 150,000 people have been laid to rest on these slopes. There are many sites commemorating the events leading to Jesus's arrest and, it's believed, his ascension to heaven.

Walk Facts

Start Dome of the Ascension

End Church of All Nations

Length 1¼km; three hours

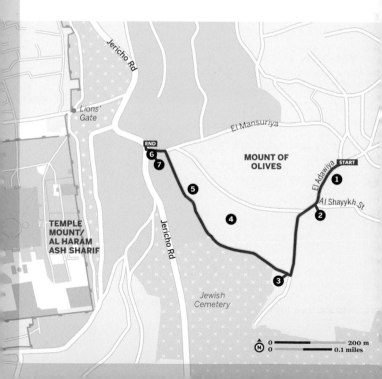

❶ Dome & Chapel of the Ascension

Get off bus 255 in front of 101 El Adawiya St and head to the entrance of the simply designed, octagon-shaped **Dome of the Ascension/Chapel of the Ascension** (5NIS; ⏰7.30-10.30am & 1.30-2.30pm). It's believed that Jesus came here to say goodbye to his disciples and ascend to heaven; a small piece of bedrock is said to bear the mark of Jesus's footprint.

❷ Church of the Pater Noster

Around 50m downhill at the intersection with Al Ghayykh St is the **Church of the Pater Noster** (☎02-626-4904; 8NIS; ⏰8.30am-noon & 2.30-4.30pm Mon-Sat Apr-Sep, from 8am Oct-Mar) where it's said Jesus preached to his disciples during the last week of his life. Roam and see the Lord's Prayer translated into 132 languages.

❸ Tomb of the Prophets

Head downhill and just before you pass the Seven Arches Hotel, turn right down two flights of steps, where you'll see a sign pointing left to the **Tomb of the Prophets** (admission 5NIS; ⏰9am-3pm Mon-Thu). The caretaker will hand you a candle and you can descend into a dark cavern where it's said prophets and their followers are buried.

❹ Church of Dominus Flevit

Once back on the main road, 25m or so on your right is the entrance to the **Church of Dominus Flevit** (☎02-626-6450; ⏰8am-11.45am & 2.30-5pm). Just inside is a two-car garage next to a fenced-in enclosure with an ossuary filled with Herodian-era bones.

❺ Russian Orthodox Convent of St Mary Magdalene

Downhill again for about 75m, the strikingly beautiful golden onions sparkling in the sunlight are part of the Russian Orthodox Convent of St Mary Magdalene (p69). Visiting hours are extremely limited so you'll likely only get a glimpse from above.

❻ Garden of Gethsemane

On the other side of the road is the entrance to the Garden of Gethsemane (p69). Biblical tradition says this was where Jesus slept his final night, prayed with his disciples, was betrayed by Judas and arrested.

❼ Church of All Nations

Next to the garden is the Church of All Nations (p67), whose glittering mosaic cupola and stone in the centre of the altar is said to be where Jesus rested. Further down the hill you can grab a taxi, or walk uphill and enter the Old City at Lions' Gate.

Jerusalem East Jerusalem

For reviews see

⊙	Sights	p66
⊗	Eating	p70
⊗	Drinking	p73
⊙	Shopping	p73

400 m
0.2 miles

Church of the Ascension

MT SCOPUS

Shmu'el Ben Adaya

Nahal Ha'egoz

Khaled

El Muqdasi St

EAST JERUSALEM

Palestinian Heritage Museum

Rockefeller Museum

As-Zahra St

Ibn Batuta

Ibn Khaldun

Abu Taleb St

Abu Obeida St

St George's Cathedral

Salah Ad Din St

Astahani

Al-Rashid St

Derekh Shchem (Nablus) Rd

Garden

Van Paassen

St George's St

Shivtei Israel

Museum on the Seam

Hayim Barlev Blvd

Shimon Ha-Tsadik

Chel Hand

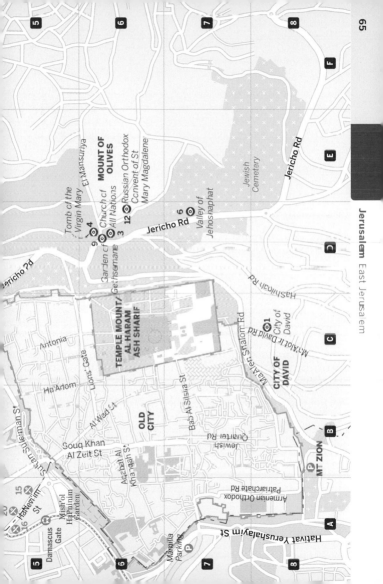

5

6

7

8

F

E

D

C

B

A

MOUNT OF OLIVES

El Mansuriya

Tomb of the Virgin Mary

4

Church of All Nations

9

Garden of Gethsemane

Russian Orthodox Convent of St Mary Magdalene

12

3

6

Valley of Jehosaphat

Jericho Rd

Jericho Rd

Jericho Rd

Jewish Cemetery

HaShiloah Rd

City of David

1

CITY OF DAVID

Mt Al Ofel David Rd

Ma'alen Shalom Rd

Antonia

TEMPLE MOUNT/ AL HARAM ASH SHARIF

Ha'Adom

Lions' Gate

Al Wad St

OLD CITY

Bas Al Silsia St

Jewish Quarter Rd

MT ZION

Souq Khan Al Zeit St

Aqabat Al Khanqah St

Armenian Orthodox Patriarchate Rd

Manqilla Parking

Hativat Yerushalayim St

Hativat Yerushalayim St

Sultan Suleiman St

15

16

HaNevi'im St

Mishol HaHufnim Garden

Damascus Gate

P

Sights

City of David ARCHAEOLOGICAL SITE

1 ⊙ MAP P64, C8

As teeming with controversy as it is with ancient history, the City of David is one of Jerusalem's most active archaeological sites. The oldest part of Jerusalem, it was a settlement during the Canaanite period; David is said to have captured the city and to have brought the Ark of the Covenant here 3000 years ago. Excavations began in the 1850s and are ongoing, as are arguments over the development and expansion of the site which many consider to be on Palestinian lands. (☑ info 02-627-4365, tour reservations 077-996-6726; www.cityofdavid.org.il; Kidron Valley; adult/child 29/15NIS, movie 13NIS, biblical city tour adult/child 65/48NIS; ⊙8am-5pm Sun-Thu, to 2pm Fri Oct-Mar, to 7pm Sun-Thu, to 4pm Fri Apr-Sep; ⊒1, 3, 38)

Museum on the Seam GALLERY

2 ⊙ MAP P64, A4

Located on the 'seam' (border) between East and West Jerusalem, this gallery presents rotating contemporary art exhibitions, often exploring themes of identity, multiplicity and faith. Expect anything from neon multimedia installations to searing recreations of biblical scenes – whatever is on display is sure to be thought provoking. The building itself served as a forward military position for the Israeli army from 1948 to 1967 and still bears the scars of war. (☑02-628-1278;

Church of All Nations and Russian Orthodox Convent of St Mary Magdalene (p69)

www.mots.org.il; 4 Chel Handasa St;
adult/student 30/25NIS; ⊙10am-5pm
Mon, Wed & Thu, to 2pm Fri, 2-8pm Tue;
🚉Shivtei Israel)

Church of All Nations CHURCH

3 ⊙ MAP P64, D6

Built above the remains of two
previous churches, this Franciscan
basilica crowns the site where
Jesus is believed to have prayed
through the night before he was
betrayed (Matthew 26:36). Inside
the church, also referred to as the
Sanctuary of the Agony of Jesus,
light is muted by stained-glass
windows and the vaulted ceiling
spangled with stars, to evoke the
mood of Jesus's nocturnal prayers
in the Garden of Gethsemane
(p69). (Basilica of Gethsemane; Mount
of Olives; ⊙8am-6pm Apr-Sep, to 5pm
Oct-Mar)

Tomb of the Virgin Mary CHRISTIAN SITE

4 ⊙ MAP P64, D6

Centuries of candle smoke have
blackened the walls of this subterranean shrine, one of Christian-
ity's holiest sites. According to
tradition, this is the resting place
of Mary, mother of Jesus. Though
strung with countless lanterns and
crowded with icons worth millions
of shekels, the space is faintly lit. A
central shrine is cloaked in velvet,
and pilgrims can duck inside.
(Mount of Olives; admission free;
⊙5am-noon & 2.30-5pm Apr-Sep,
from 6am Oct-Mar)

Palestinian Heritage Museum MUSEUM

5 ⊙ MAP P64, B3

Within a school complex (the Dar
Al Tifil Al Arabi Institute) in a 19th-
century building, this museum provides a useful primer on ancient
and modern Palestinian culture.
Displays on embroidery, basket
weaving and agrarian implements
offer a glimpse into age-old village traditions. The museum also
details the displacement of the
Palestinian people, including lists
of formerly Arab villages, and me-
morialises events such as the 1948
Deir Yassin massacre. Those striv-
ing to understand this complex
region shouldn't miss a visit here.
(Dar Al Tifel Al Arabi Institute; ☏02-
627-2531; www.dartifl.org; Abu Obaidah
St; adult/child 20/10NIS; ⊙8am-3pm
Mon-Wed & Sat, to 4pm Thu)

Valley of Jehoshaphat RELIGIOUS SITE

6 ⊙ MAP P64, D7

The word *jehoshaphat* (*yeho-
shafat* in Hebrew) means 'God has
judged', and this narrow furrow
of land located between Temple
Mount/Al Haram Ash Sharif and
the Mount of Olives is where it is
said the events of Judgment Day
will take place (Joel 3:12) and
all nations will be judged. At the
southern end is a series of tombs
dating from the Second Temple
period. (Jericho Rd, Kidron Valley; by
donation; ⊙daylight hours)

Garden Tomb entrance

Garden Tomb
GARDENS

7  MAP P64, A4

Away from the din of Derekh Shchem (Nablus) Rd is a tranquil patch of green, considered by its trustees to be the garden and sepulchre of Joseph of Arimathea, and possibly the place where Jesus was resurrected. The claims are strongly disputed, but this walled and attractively landscaped space is more conducive to contemplation than the teeming Church of the Holy Sepulchre (p38), the site more widely believed to be that of the crucifixion. There are some interesting archaeological excavations here, too. (📞02-539-8100; www.gardentomb.org; Conrad Schick St; admission free; ⏰8am-6pm Mon-Sat; 🚌Damascus Gate)

Rockefeller Museum
MUSEUM

8 MAP P64, C4

The Rockefeller Museum doesn't ride high on must-see lists for Jerusalem, but it's calm, uncrowded and only a short walk from Herod's Gate. The atmosphere is as enjoyable as the contents; make for the **Cloisters**, where Roman-era antiquities are arranged around a gushing water feature. Other highlights include 9th-century mosaics, Roman ossuary vessels and Byzantine-era blocks featuring early Christian inscriptions. (📞02-670-8074; 27 Sultan Suleiman St; admission free; ⏰10am-3pm Sun, Mon, Wed & Thu, to 2pm Sat; 🚌1, 3 & 51, 🚌Damascus Gate)

Garden of Gethsemane

GARDENS

9 ⊙ MAP P64, D6

After a night of feverish prayer, Jesus is believed to have been arrested in this garden (Mark 14:26, 32–50), now attached to the Church of All Nations (p67). It has some of the world's oldest olive trees (in Hebrew *gat shmanim* means 'oil press'), though testing has failed to prove conclusively that these were the same trees beneath which Jesus prayed and his disciples slept. A railing protects the remaining trees from visitors (scotching pilgrims' attempts to snap off branches). (Mount of Olives; admission free; ☉8.30am-noon & 2.30-5pm Mon-Wed, Fri & Sat, to 4pm Thu & Sun)

Church of the Ascension

CHURCH

10 ⊙ MAP P64, F4

In 1898 the Ottomans granted Germany 8 hectares of land on the Mount of Olives. This was set aside for a church and hospice, and the complex was named after Augusta Victoria, wife of Kaiser Wilhelm II. Completed in 1910, the church is decorated with mosaics and frescoes, and has a 60m-high bell tower that can be climbed by visitors (there are 203 steps). (www.evangelisch-in-jerusalem.org; cnr Anbar & Martin Buber Sts, Mount of Olives; admission 5NIS; ☉8am-1pm Mon-Sat; 🚌275)

St George's Cathedral

CHURCH

11 ⊙ MAP P64, A3

Named after the patron saint of England, who is traditionally believed to have been martyred in Palestine in the early 4th century, St George's Cathedral was consecrated in 1898 and has a mixed Arabic- and English-speaking congregation. The church compound is a piece of the British Mandate frozen in time, featuring symbols of the British presence in Jerusalem including a font given by Queen Victoria, memorials to British servicemen and a tower built in memory of King Edward VII. (www.j-diocese.org; Derekh Shchem (Nablus) Rd; ☉hours vary; 🚌Shivtei Israel)

Russian Orthodox Convent of St Mary Magdalene

CHURCH

12 ⊙ MAP P64, D6

A glint of St Petersburg on the Mount of Olives, this shapely church was constructed in the style of a 17th-century Russian Orthodox church. Built in 1888 by Alexander III in memory of his mother, the church is now a convent and guards the relics of two Russian saints. Its seven golden onion-shaped domes form one of Jerusalem's most attractive and surprising landmarks. (Mount of Olives; ☉10am-noon Tue & Thu)

Church of the Pater Noster (p63)

Eating

View Cafe Bar MIDDLE EASTERN $$$

13 🍴 MAP P64, C4

The View Cafe Bar, East Jerusalem's only rooftop restaurant, serves up Palestinian cuisine alongside a spectacular Old City view. Go for a sundowner to welcome the evening, but stay for the worthwhile dinner. Don't miss the creative takes on traditional Palestinian dishes, such as the mini sandwich versions of *musakhan* (seasoned meat served on a bed of bread, onions, oil and sumac). (📞02-628-4841; www.facebook.com/TheViewJerusalem; 6 Rashid St, Holy Land Hotel; mains 50-125NIS; 🕙2-11pm)

Azzahra Restaurant MEDITERRANEAN $$

14 🍴 MAP P64, B4

In a quiet corner close to the Old City, Azzahra is an ideal place for a group or family looking for something familiar – fresh and satisfying pizza. The restaurant offers up a range of Middle Eastern, Mediterranean and French dishes, including pastas and fillet mignon, but the real deal is the brick-oven, thin-crust Italian pizza. (📞02-628-2447; www.azzahrahotel.com/restaurant.html; 13 Azzahra St, Azzahra Hotel; pizzas 45-75NIS; 🕙noon-11pm)

Al Ayed
MIDDLE EASTERN $

15 ⊗ MAP P64, A5

Hands down, the best lamb kebab sandwich for the money in Jerusalem. The falafel and hummus and other specialities like barbecue chicken with salads and lamb with rice aren't bad either. Bustling place with attentive service just outside Damascus Gate. (☏02-628-2182; 2 Hanevi'm St; mains 13-35NIS; ☺24hr; ☎)

Restaurant Fish
SEAFOOD $$$

16 ⊗ MAP P64, A5

With uniformed waitstaff and white tablecloths, the Restaurant Fish is refined for a bus-station-adjacent spot. Tasty calamari and shrimp (fried, grilled or with tabasco sauce), crabs, mussels are options for starters, and delicious fresh whole snapper, sea bass, salmon and mullet come prepared in a variety of ways. Rib-eye and lamb chops are also on the menu. There's outdoor seating on a pleasant covered patio. (East Jerusalem Fish; ☏02-585-5590; cnr Ha'Nevi'im & Chel Handassa Sts; mains 70-100NIS; ☺1-10pm)

Sarwa Street Kitchen
MIDDLE EASTERN $$

17 ⊗ MAP P64, A3

Sarwa Street Kitchen is a chill place to loiter with a quiet coffee, juice, meal or beer. The kitchen offers a range of freshly prepared dishes, from homemade pizzas and burritos to Palestinian favourites such

as *makloubeh* (chicken, rice, vegetables and spices cooked together and turned 'upside down'), as well as vegan and vegetarian options. (www.facebook.com/sarwa streetkitchen; 42 Salah Ad Din St; mains 38-55NIS; ☺10am-11pm Sat-Thu; ☎⬛; ⬛Shivtei Israel)

Al Mihbash
MIDDLE EASTERN $$

18 ⊗ MAP P64, A4

Perch on an overhanging balcony table for a feast of Palestinian-style dishes, from fish kebabs and falafel to stuffed chicken, along with enough Mediterranean salmon fillets and steaks to keep homesick expats happy. Smashed avocado and almond smoothies also feature on the somewhat scattered menu. Service is perfunctory, but food (and views) are great. (☏02-628-9185; www.facebook.com/AlMihbashRestaurantAndCafe; 21 Derekh Shchem (Nablus) Rd; mains 50-75NIS; ☺10am-late; ⬛Shivtei Israel)

Nordic Café
CAFE $$

19 ⊗ MAP P64, B4

The relatively chic and cosy Scandinavian-themed Nordic Café is a perfect place to stop for a coffee, fresh juice cocktail, pretty pastries or freshly prepared pasta, sandwich or salad. Better yet; it's one of the few (if only) sources for fresh Finnish bread in Jerusalem. (☏02-627-4626; www.facebook.com/NordicCafeJerusalem; 9 As Zahra St; mains 29-38NIS; ☺9am-10pm; ☎; ⬛Shivtei Israel)

Kaak bread

Al Amin Sweets & Bakery

BAKERY $

20  MAP P64, A5

Al Amin Bakery brings Jerusalem together to literally break bread. On any given day Palestinians, Israelis, Ethiopians, Filipinos and tourists of all kinds pass through this Palestinian-owned shop close to Damascus Gate for some signature Jerusalem *kaak* (circular toasted bread) or baked goods filled with meat, cheese or *zaatar* (a blend of spices that includes hyssop, sumac and sesame), among other homemade specialities. (☎02-628-8334; 14 HaNeve'im St; pastries 5-10NIS; ☺6am-10pm; 🚊Damascus Gate)

Courtyard Restaurant

MIDDLE EASTERN $$$

21 MAP P64, A3

Even if you're not staying at the American Colony Hotel, it's worth stopping by the Courtyard Restaurant for Middle Eastern dishes served on tiled tables beneath the shade of olive trees. Try the *mahshi* (rice-stuffed courgettes). It's a little pricey, but the pretty setting makes it worth the splurge. (American Colony Hotel, 1 Louis Vincent St; mains 65-115NIS; ☺6.30am-11pm)

Al Diwan Restaurant

MIDDLE EASTERN $$$

22 🐾 MAP P64, B1

It feels pricey if you've been snacking on street food all day, but the restaurant at the Ambassador is one of East Jerusalem's best places to eat. Puffy pita breads emerge from the charcoal-fired oven and are heaped onto tables alongside smoky grilled meats, green wheat soup and great pizzas. Rather than the so-so dining room, enjoy this bounty on the verandah. (📞 02-541-2222; www.jerusalemambassador.com; Ambassador Hotel, 5 Derekh Shchem (Nablus) Rd; mains 70-120NIS; ⏱ noon-11pm; 🚇 Shimon Ha-Tsadik)

Drinking

Cellar Bar

BAR

23 🍷 MAP P64, A3

The bar at the legendary American Colony Hotel looks very Jerusalem with vaulted ceilings, stone floors and windowless walls, just like one of the Old City's chapels or crypts. The atmosphere, however, is lively, with a mix of journalists, international aid types, Palestinian and Arab businesspeople, wealthy foreign tourists and simply those interested in a stiff cocktail in a historical setting. (1 Louis Vincent St, American Colony Hotel; ⏱ 5pm-midnight)

Shopping

Educational Bookshop & Cafe

BOOKS

24 🔒 MAP P64, B4

The only English-language bookstore in East Jerusalem, the Educational Bookshop attracts journalists, aid workers, activists and intellectuals. There's a range of books and DVDs with a neutral or pro-Palestinian perspective on the Arab-Israeli conflict, and a good selection of novels, magazines and Palestinian music CDs. Linger in the tiny upstairs cafe for a tea, a sandwich or a chat. (📞 02 628-3704; www.educationalbookshop. com; 19 Salah Ad Din St; ⏱ 9am-8pm; 🛜; 🚇 Shivtei Israel)

Sunbula

ARTS & CRAFTS

26 🔒 MAP P64, B1

This non-profit outfit empowers Palestinian artisans by promoting and selling traditional handicrafts, including embroidery, basketry, weaving, carving and olive-oil soap. It runs two shops in Jerusalem, one of which is inside the St Andrew's Scottish Guesthouse and the other here in East Jerusalem. All of the items for sale are handmade (📞 02-672-1707; www.sunbula. org; 15 Derekh Shchem (Nablus) Rd, ⏱ noon-6pm Mon-Thu & Sat; 🚇 Shimon Ha-Tsadik)

Explore ✦
Downtown Jerusalem

A few blocks west of the Old City, Jerusalem's downtown hums with bars, brunch spots and boutiques. Threaded with car-free streets, it attracts locals and tourists who dawdle their way from shops to sun-bleached plazas. Stone-flanked alleys, featuring jewellers, art studios, courtyard cafes and souvenir shops, are tucked away where traffic can't reach, branching off from pedestrian drag Ben Yehuda.

What downtown Jerusalem lacks in major sights is made up for with a wealth of dining and drinking experiences. Come hungry and spend your time dabbling in the international cuisine and spirits scene at Mahane Yehuda Market (p76). One of its best restaurants is, appropriately enough, called Machneyuda (p84). Afterwards, make a night of sampling brews at Beer Bazaar (p87), or just wander the market's aisles and see what you get into – this is one of the city's hottest nightlife spots, with a lively bar scene that spills over into the streets.

Getting There & Around

Jerusalem's light-rail line cuts through the heart of downtown on Yaffa St with stops at City Hall, King George and Mahane Yehuda, among others.

🚌 Many bus lines criss-cross the area.

Downtown Jerusalem Map on p80

Backgammon in Mahane Yehuda Market (p76) CHAMELEONSEYE/SHUTTERSTOCK ©

Top Experience 📷

Take a tasting tour of Mahane Yehuda Market

Let your tastebuds travel the world along the narrow streets that make up Mahane Yehuda Market. Be tempted by Georgian baked goods, Iraqi stuffed vine leaves, Argentinian empanadas, homemade Italian limoncello, Yemenite remedy drinks, Japanese sushi and, of course, falafel. The menu at this market of 350 shops, the city's best, would thrill the most demanding appetite.

◉ MAP P80, F2

www.machne.co.il

Jaffa Rd

🕐 market stalls 8am-7pm Sun-Thu, 9am-3pm Fri, restaurants & bars open late

🚊 Mahane Yehuda

Guided Tasting Tours

A growing number of tours are available if you want to add some structure, insight and expertise to your market visit. Trained chef and owner of The Atelier, **Tali Friedman** (🍴02-537-0666; http://haatelie.com/en; groups up to 15 people 9500NIS), leads small groups, stopping for samples and providing suggestions of where to buy the best of everything. The tour ends sipping local wine at The Atelier, her cooking school space with views of the market below.

Other group tour options are Yalla Basta (https://en.machne.co.il/category/classic-tour) and American expatriate Joel Haber (www.funjoelisrael.com). Cost depends on group numbers.

Speciality Shops

Like other markets, Mahane Yehuda has 'ordinary' businesses like barbers, flower shops, housewares and pharmacies. Convenient, sure. But it's the speciality food shops and restaurants, the kaleidoscopic displays of spices, the towering piles of fruit and the rows of simmering cauldrons that are the main draw here.

A handful of favourites includes the following:

Tzidkiyahu (79 Etz Chaim St) For olives.

Halva Kingdom (p90) For halva (sweet made from sesame or tahini base, mixed with variety of flavours).

Azura (p84) For stuffed vegetables and sofrito (tomato, onion and garlic base for a stew).

Ishtabach (🍴02-623-2997; cnr Shikma St & Beit Ya'akov St; mains 44-63NIS; ⏰noon-1am; 🚋Mahane Yehuda) For shamburak (Kurdish pastry stuffed with various meats or vegetables).

Diwiny Pita Bar (p85) Not your run-of-the-mill stuffed pitas; these have creative veg and meat fillings.

Morduch (p86) For kibbeh (meat-filled cracked wheat croquettes).

★ Top Tips

◦ Friday afternoons can be positively overwhelming because of preparations for Shabbat. Mornings from Monday to Wednesday, while not quiet, are not as busy.

◦ Visit at least twice – once before noon and once in the evening to experience the market's changing atmosphere. You'll also want to eat here more than once!

◦ Mornings have mostly local shoppers, as do the minutes before closing. Prices are also cheapest at these times.

◦ When shop owners pull down shutters at night, check out the graffiti; more than 100 pieces in all, done by a group of young religious Jews from Brooklyn.

✕ Take a Break

On nearby Beit Ya'akov, Hachapuria (p85) serves emroli, a Georgian speciality of puffy bread filled with a choice of cheese, beans, spinach and potatoes.

Walking Tour 🥾

Mahane Yehuda for Foodies

A walk through Mahane Yehuda's alleyways, lined with speciality food stalls and sit-down restaurants, gives you a taste of the city's rich ethnic diversity.

Walk Facts

Start Corner Jaffa & Beit Ya'acov Sts

End Corner Agrippas & Etz HaChaim Sts

Length 1km; two hours

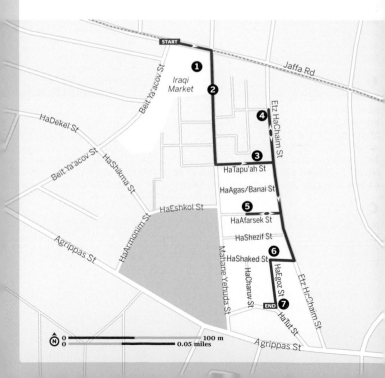

❶ Iraqi Market

Just down the stairs in HaHamrot Sq you'll find what's known as the **Iraqi Market**, named for the Iraqi Jews who founded the area in the early 1930s. Old-timers meet here to play backgammon, gossip and sip tea and coffee.

❷ Mahane Yehuda St

Head down **Mahane Yehuda St**, one of the market's two main stretches, for a little more (though not by much) elbow room. This open-air street, lined with clothing and accessories shops, as well as delis, butchers, and pickle and spice stalls, is a good introduction to the dizzying variety

❸ Ochlim B'shuk

Make a left onto HaTapu'ah St for a gander at the locals' action at several fish and butcher shops. Stop at **Ochlim B'shuk**, at 8 HaTapua'h, where Persian-, Moroccan- and Kurdish-style soups are usually simmering in kerosene-heated cauldrons.

❹ Kingdom of Halva

Next, head left, back north on Etz HaChaim St, the other major market alleyway. You can't miss the **Kingdom of Halva**, which sells more than 100 varieties of the sweet treat made from tahini.

❺ Yazidi Spice Shop

Turn around south on Etz Ha-Chaim and then right onto narrow HaAfarsek St, which in addition to a few ordinary housewares shops has the **Yazidi Spice Shop** on 11 HaAfarsek St. Opened by a family of Iranian immigrants in 2003, it sells medicinal herbs meant to treat nearly every ailment. The owner's sister supplies the shop with many spices brought from Iran, where she still lives.

❻ Mizrachi Pitzuchim

Continue south on either Mahane Yehuda or Etz HaChaim and then turn onto HaShaked St; at 9 HaShaked is **Mizrachi Pitzuchim** where you can sample nuts, dried fruits, chocolates and pastries

❼ Etrog Man

Near Agrippas on HaEgoz St is the **Etrog Man** (www.etrogman.com; HaEgoz St, Mahane Yehuda Market; ⊙8am-sunset Sun-Thu, 9am-2pm Fri; 🚊Mahane Yehuda) who doles out healthy juice concoctions, including citron, quince and sugarcane and can personalise medicinal drinks upon request.

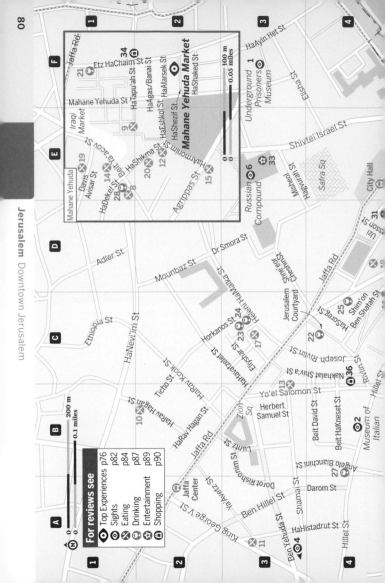

Etz HaChaim St **34**

21

Jaffa Rd

Mahane Yehuda St

HaTapu'ah St

HaAgas/Banai St

HaAfarsek St

Mahane Yehuda Market

HaShaked St

9

HaShezif St

HaEshkol St

Iraqi
Market

19

Mahane
Yehuda

Davis
Avisar St

14

28

8

HaDekel St

Beit Ya'acov St

HaShikma St

HaCarmon St

HaShezif St

12

20

15

Agrippas St

100 m
0.05 miles

Underground 1
Prisoners
Museum

HaAyin Het St

Elisha St

Shivtei Israel St

Russian 6
Compound

33

Misheol St

Hagura St

Safra Sq

City Hall

Adler St

Mounbaz St

Dr Smora St

Ethiopia St

HaNevi'im St

Ticho St

HaRav Kook St

Helení HaMalka St

Shriejor
Chesnisus

Jaffa Rd

Uzi
Nissim St

31

9

Jerusalem
Courtyard

22

Shim'on
Ben Shatah St

HaSoreg St

25

HaRav Hagan St

10

Horkanos St **24**

23

Elyashar St

HaHatzelet St

Bejshar St

17

Nakhalat Shiv'a St

Joseph Rivlin St

36

Rivlin St

Hillel St

Zion
Sq

Yo'el Salomon St

13

Herbert
Samuel St

Beit David St

Museum of 2
Italian

Jaffa Rd

Jaffa Center

Ya'avetz St

Dorot Rishonim St

Luntz St

Beit HaKneset St

Angelo Bianchini St

27

Darom St

King George V St

Ben Hillel St

Shamai St

Ben Yehuda St

4

11

HaHistadrut St

Hillel St

200 m
0.1 miles

N

For reviews see

◉ Top Experiences p76
◉ Sights p82
✗ Eating p84
🍷 Drinking p87
✪ Entertainment p89
🛍 Shopping p90

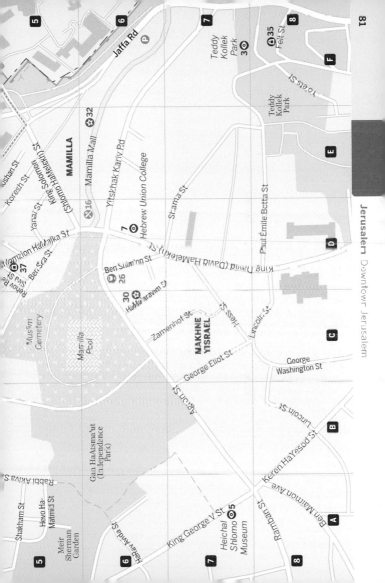

5

6

Jaffa Rd

Kushan St

Koresh St

MAMILLA

Yanai St

King Solomon St (Shlomo HaMelekh)

★ 32

Mamilla Mall

✕ 16

Yitshak Kariv Rd

Hebrew Union College

7 ⊙

(Romzion HaMalka St

37

Ben Sra St

Rehov Ha...

Sira St

Ben Shimon St

26 ⊙

30 ⊙

HaMa'aravim C

Strama St

King David (David HaMelekh) St

Muslim Cemetery

Mamilla Pool

Zamenhof St

MAKHNE YISRAEL

Hess St

Lincoln St

George Eliot St

Agron St

George Washington St

Lincoln St

Teddy Kollek Park

3 ⊙

7

Teddy Kollek Park

Paul Émile Botta St

Yo'el St

35

Feit St

8

F

E

D

C

Keren HaYesod St

B

Ben Maimon Ave

Ramban St

A

Gan HaAtsma'ut (Independence Park)

Rabbi Akiva St

Shakham St

Hevo Ha-Matmid St

Meir Sherman Garden

HaRav Avida St

King George V St

Heichal Shlomo Museum

5 ⊙

7

8

5

6

Sights

Underground Prisoners Museum
MUSEUM

1 ⊙ MAP P80, F3

Few travellers are aware of this fascinating museum about the struggle of the Jewish underground's efforts to oust the British and create Israel. It's tucked behind the City Hall complex (next to the future site of the Bezalel Academy of Arts & Design) and housed in what was Jerusalem's central prison during the British mandate; it was previously used as storage and office space for decades. Various cells are reconstructed to tell the story of the prisoners' struggles and punishment. (☏02-623-3166; hamachtarot_jerusalem@mod.gov.il; 1 Misheol Hagvurah St, Russian Compound; adult/child 15/10NIS; ☺9am-5pm Sun-Thu)

Museum of Italian Jewish Art
MUSEUM

2 ⊙ MAP P80, B4

A baroque-style synagogue, twinkling with gold vine leaves and decorative arches, is the focal point of this overlooked museum. Transported across the Mediterranean piece by piece from its place of origin, Conegliano in the region of Veneto in Italy, the synagogue was reconstructed here in 1951. Within the same building is a collection of objects associated with Jewish life in Italy, from the Renaissance period through to the present day. (☏02-624-1610; www.ijamuseum.org; 25 Hillel St; adult/child 25/15NIS; ☺10.30am-4.30pm Sun-Wed, noon-7pm Thu; 🚌Jaffa Center)

Teddy Kollek Park
PARK

3 ⊙ MAP P80, F7

Kids frolic in the fountains to cool off on hot days, and families picnic on the lawn just outside Jaffa Gate (p50) and next to the Artists' Colony (p90). Stone walls detail important events in the life of Kollek, who was mayor of Jerusalem for 30 years. 'Dancing fountain' shows happen on weekday evenings in summer at 8pm, 9pm and 10pm. (near Mamilla Ave; ☺7am-11pm)

Ades Synagogue
SYNAGOGUE

4 ⊙ MAP P80, A3

Built by the Syrian Halebi Congregation in 1901, this synagogue was named for Ovadia and Yosef Ades, the Aleppo brothers who financed the project. It quickly became a centre for Syrian *hazzanut* (Jewish liturgical singing) and saw the training of many a Jerusalem cantor. Today it maintains the rare tradition of *bakashot,* a set cycle of Kabbalistic poetry sung in the early hours of Shabbat during the winter months. (cnr Be'ersheva & Shilo Sts; ☺hours vary)

Heichal Shlomo Museum
JEWISH SITE

5 ⊙ MAP P80, A7

The severe-looking building on King George V St is the 1950s-designed seat of the Chief Rabbinate of Israel, and now home to the Wolfson Museum's galleries of Jewish art. This vast complex was designed in the 1950s and styled along the lines of Solomon's Temple – Heichal Shlomo literally means 'Solomon's Mansion'. Check out the semicircular balcony, intended for the use of the Chief Rabbi as he addressed throngs of believers. (Wolfson Museum of Jewish Art; ☎02-588-9010; www.eng. hechalshlomo.org.il; 58 King George V St, museum & rooftop adult/child 20/15NIS; ☺9am-3pm Sun-Tue & Thu)

Russian Compound HISTORIC SITE

6 ◉ MAP P80, F3

Dominated by the green domes of its **Church of the Holy Trinity**, this compound was acquired by the Russian Orthodox Church in 1860 to strengthen the Russian imperial presence in the Holy Land. In the last years of the British Mandate, it and nearby streets were turned into a fortified administrative zone nicknamed 'Bevingrad' by Palestinian Jews after the reviled British foreign secretary Ernest Bevin. (Shivtei Israel St; ☺Church of the Holy Trinity 9am-1pm & 3-6pm Tue, Wed & Thu, to 1pm Fri, 7.30-noon & 4.30-7.30pm Sat, 8.30-1pm Sun Apr-Sep, 9am-1pm Mon-Fri, to noon Sat Oct-Mar; 🚌City Hall)

Hebrew Union College ARCHITECTURE

7 ◉ MAP P80, D6

With a conical glass roof feature, the Reform Movement's educational

Teddy Kollek Park

and cultural complex is an arresting feature of Jerusalem's downtown skyline. Part of the centre's design was conceived by Moshe Safdie, whose architecture also graces Mamilla Mall and Yad Vashem. (Beit Shmuel; www.beitshmuel.co.il; 6 Eliyahu Shama St)

Eating

Machneyuda   INTERNATIONAL $$$

8 🍴 MAP P80, E1

Is it New York comfort food, Italian fine dining or haute cuisine? This superb restaurant owned by three of Israel's most acclaimed chefs near Mahane Yehuda Market has won local acclaim for its playful menu, which offers Catalan-style calamari, black linguine with crab and good ol' fashioned steak and potatoes. Book well in advance, and pray there's semolina cake. (📞02-533-3442; www.machneyuda. co.il; 10 Beit Ya'akov St; mains 86-175NIS, tasting menu 295NIS; 🕐12.30-4pm & 6.30-11pm Sun-Thu, to 3pm Fri; 🚊Mahane Yehuda)

Azura   MIDDLE EASTERN $$

9 🍴 MAP P80, E1

With slow-cooked comfort food, on kerosene burners no less, and efficient service, this Turkish-influenced kosher restaurant off Rehov HaEshkol St near Mahane Yehuda Market is one of Jerusalem's best loved. The fragrance of goulash and meatballs is enough to set stomachs rumbling, while the signature dish – aubergine stuffed with cinnamon-scented minced beef and pine nuts – is peppery, filling and served at lightning speed. (📞02-623-5204; 4 Ha Eshkol, Iraqi Market; mains 22-100NIS; 🕐9.30am-4pm Sun-Fri; 🖋; 🚊Mahane Yehuda)

Anna   ITALIAN $$$

10 🍴 MAP P80, B2

On the upper floor of elegant Ticho House, Anna is a stylish spot for a coffee or an Italian meal. Nibble pastries, *pizza bianca,* linguine with mushrooms and truffle oil, stuffed sea bream or artichoke omelette, content with the knowledge that it's for a good cause: the cafe employs and trains local youth in distress. (📞02-543-4144; www.annarest.co.il; Ticho House, 10 HaRav Hagan St; mains 72-106NIS; 🕐9am-11pm Sun-Thu, to 2pm Fri; 🖋; 🚊Jaffa Center)

Pinati   MIDDLE EASTERN $$

11 🍴 MAP P80, A3

While locals swear by the hummus, served with pita and piquant garlic-chilli paste, this hole-in-the-wall's well-seasoned mains are also worth sampling: slow-stewed moussaka, schnitzels, bean soups and shakshuka (a rich egg-and-tomato breakfast dish). Casual dining and comforting kosher food are a winning formula, so you may have to battle crowds at lunchtime for one of the few tiny tables. (📞02-625-4540; http://pinati.co.il; 13 King George V St; mains 25-60NIS; 🕐8am-7pm Sun-Thu, to 3pm Fri; 🖋; 🚊Jaffa Center)

Ottolenghi's Jerusalem

Jerusalem-born chef, author and television presenter Yotam Ottolenghi is an unofficial but highly influential ambassador for the city's culinary heritage. His cookbook *Jerusalem* showcases culinary combinations that he describes as 'belonging to specific groups but also belonging to everybody else'. Proving this point is the fact that Ottolenghi, who is Jewish from West Jerusalem, and co-author Sami Tamimi, a Palestinian from East Jerusalem, grew up eating slightly different versions of the same dishes. A number of our favourite traditional restaurants and pastry shops are profiled in the book, including Abu Shukri (p53) and Azura (p84).

Hachapuria   GEORGIAN $$

12 🌀 MAP P80, E2

Hachapuria serves up sizzlingly delicious Georgian food, the most famous being its namesake *hachapuri*, a triangle of dough filled with egg and cheese (and spinach if you'd like). Located on the perimeter of Mahane Yehuda Market (p76), the restaurant is simple in decor but holds its own as it stands next to some of Jerusalem's best bars and dessert spots. (☏02-537-3630; www.facebook.com/hachapuria; cnr Shikma St & Eshkol St; mains 25-35NIS; ⏱9am-9pm Sun-Thu; ☏; 🚇Mahane Yehuda)

T'mol Shilshom   CAFE $$

13 🌀 MAP P80, B3

Whether you settle into the book-lined interior or the shaded courtyard, T'mol Shilshom is one of Jerusalem's most relaxing brunch spots. This friendly kosher joint is best known for its shakshuka: classic, spicy or cheese-laden versions

of the Middle Eastern egg and-tomato bake are on offer, always with a mountain of fresh bread, salad and olive tapenade. (☏02-623-2758; www.tmol-shilshom.co.il; 5 Yo'el Salomon St; mains 40-55NIS; ⏱8.30am-midnight Sun-Thu, to 2pm Fri, after Shabbat-midnight Sat; ☏🖊; 🚇Jaffa Center)

Diwiny Pita Bar   ISRAELI $$

14 🌀 MAP P80, E1

Good luck finding a seat at this cool little spot just outside Mahane Yehuda Market. It specialises in stuffing pitas with seasonal unconventional fare like crispy cauliflower, osso buco and ceviche. It's mouthwatering and messy – you'll need the roll of paper towels to clean off. The side of 'three stage fries', onion rings, potatoes, tomatoes and scallions in aioli sauce is excellent. (6 Beit Ya'akov St, Mahane Yehuda Market; mains 30-42NIS; ⏱noon-midnight Sun-Wed, to 2am Thu, to 4pm Fri, 8pm-1am Sat; 🖊)

Morduch

MIDDLE EASTERN $$

15 🔀 MAP P80, E2

Kibbeh, *kibbeh* and more *kibbeh*. Traditionally this Iraqi-Kurdidsh soup is made from beets, tomatoes, carrots and doughy balls stuffed with ground beef, and, of course, Morduch, which has been doling this out since 1982, does it well. Other varieties to try include those with okra, courgette and slow-roasted beef. The well-rounded menu, best for sharing, also includes a variety of stuffed vegetables, meatballs, kebabs, couscous, and chicken and beef sofrito. (📞02-624-5169; 70 Agrippas St, Mahane Yehuda Market; mains 22-62NIS; 🕑8am-5pm Sun-Thu, to 4pm Fri)

Mamilla Rooftop Restaurant

INTERNATIONAL $$$

16 🔀 MAP P80, D6

Not keen on bumping elbows with fellow diners in the Old City hummus restaurants? This sleek rooftop brasserie is a refined place to retreat. Meals (all kosher) are designed for distinguished palates, with citrus salmon sashimi, gnocchi with black olives, and roast goose accented with chocolate and caramel sauce. Reserve ahead. (📞02-548-2230; www.mamillahotel.comrooftop; 11 King Solomon (Shlomo HaMelekh) St, Mamilla; mains 92-212NIS; 🕑6pm-11pm Sun-Thu, noon-4pm Fri, noon-11pm Sat; 🚊City Hall)

Cafe Bastet

VEGETARIAN $$

17 🔀 MAP P80, C3

Hip Cafe Bastet is a queer- and vegetarian-friendly cafe and restaurant. It's open on Shabbat and is equally loved for its sandwiches (the sweet potato and mushroom with red onions and pesto is excellent) and salads as well as strong coffee and the famous vegan hot chocolate. (📞02-970-1710; https://cafe-bastet.business.site; 5 Heleni HaMalka; mains 32-42NIS; 🕑8am-11pm; 🛜🚭)

Hamarakia

SOUP $

18 🔀 MAP P80, D4

Somewhere between homey and ramshackle, this Jerusalem institution specialises in nourishing soups, which change daily. Leek, lentil and tomato are in frequent rotation, and there are always vegan options. For more than a liquid lunch, Hamarakia serves aubergine salads, hummus and other veggie dishes. The long shared table and open kitchen create a sociable atmosphere, and there's a patio out back. (📞02-625-7797; 4 Koresh St; mains from 30NIS; 🕑noon-late Sun-Thu, from 8.30pm Sat; 🚭; 🚊City Hall)

Bardak Pizza & Beer

PIZZA $$

19 🔀 MAP P80, E1

Bardak is famous in Jerusalem not just for its pizza and wide selection of beers, but also for its pizzas 'dedicated' to the city's various neighbourhoods. For example, hippie Nachalot's pizza is replete

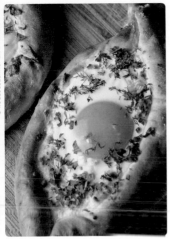

Hachapuri

nice bar help make it one of Mahane Yehuda's hottest spots. (www.facebook.com/gotcrave; 1 Shikma St, Mahane Yehuda Market; mains 43-76NIS; ⊘noon-midnight Sun-Thu, to 3.30pm Fri, 9.30pm-1am Sat)

Drinking

Beer Bazaar
CRAFT BEER

21 😊 MAP P80, F1

Glug your way through more than 100 craft beers (including dozens of Israeli brews) at this popular bar in Mahane Yehuda Market. The Jerusalem branch of Tel Aviv microbrew chain Beer Bazaar rotates both the beers on tap and the entertainment, which ranges from 'beer yoga' to live music. (☏02-671-2559; www.facebook.com/Beer.Bazaar.Jerusalem; 3 Haetz Ha'em St, Mahane Yehuda Market; ⊘11am-late Sun-Thu, to 5pm Fri, from 8pm Sat; 🚇Mahane Yehuda)

Barood
BAR

22 😊 MAP P80, C4

Pass the time beautifully at this intimate bar-restaurant in a courtyard behind Jaffa Rd while sampling from the solid selection of local wine, cocktails and delicious Balkan-meets-Italian nibbles. Red-checked tablecloths and stone walls decorated with wistful European posters make you imagine, for a split second, that you're in a Parisian bistro – though why would you want to be anywhere else? (☏02-625-9081; www.facebook.com/BaroodJerusalem; 31 Jaffa Rd; ⊘noon-late; 🚇Jaffa Center)

with aubergine, the upscale Talbiya neighbourhood has smoked salmon and ginger, while the Mahane Yehuda pizza brings a big dose of cheese and spice. (www.habardak.co.il; 4 Beit Ya'akov St; pizzas 40-75NIS; ⊘1pm-late Sun-Thu, 5-11pm Sat; 🚇Mahane Yehuda)

Crave
INTERNATIONAL $$

20 😊 MAP P80, E2

Mixing culinary influences with strict Jewish dietary laws isn't easy, but thanks to the chef-driven edgy ambition here kosher has never tasted so good. The menu is best experienced by sampling different dishes, versions of gourmet street food like a Korean noodle bowl, Philly-style burrito and tacos. Graffiti-covered brick walls and a

Kadosh

Videopub

GAY

23 🚇 MAP P80, C3

The local LGBTIQ+ community flocks to this teensy space above Cassette Bar for drinking, dancing and the occasional drag show (Thursday and Saturday are particularly busy). Expect nostalgic electronica, '80s pop tunes and a crowd welcoming of LGBTIQ+ patrons and their hetero friends. (https://sites.google.com/site/video pubjerusalem; 1st fl, 1 Horkanus St; ⏱8pm-4am Mon-Thu, Sat & Sun, from 10pm Fri; 🚊Jaffa Center)

Cassette Bar

BAR

24 🚇 MAP P80, C3

Accessed from the street (look for the metal door covered with old cassette tapes) or through the rear of the Record Bar next door, this pint-sized cave-like bar is a long-standing hipster haunt. The crowd drinks well into the night, serenaded by alternative tracks. (HaCasetta; 1 Horkanos St; ⏱8pm-5am Sat-Thu, 2pm-6am Fri; 🚊Jaffa Center)

Kadosh

CAFE

25 🚇 MAP P80, C4

Since 1967, Kadosh has been cultivating an uncanny miniature Paris, from the burnished colour scheme and outdoor seating to the intellectual chit-chat mingling with French *chansons* on the sound system. The espresso on ice with vanilla is a refresher with bite, and coffee cups are swapped for cocktail flutes when the sun goes down. (🖉02-625-4210; 6 Shlomzion

HaMalka St; ⏰7am-12.30am Sun-Thu, to 1 hour before Shabbat Fri; 📶; 🚊City Hall)

Garden Terrace

BAR

26 🚇 MAP P80, D6

Crowning one of the city's most luxurious hotels is this circular rooftop bar with, you guessed it, spectacular views. Settle into a comfy seat and order a stiff drink shaken by suspender-clad bartenders. It's welcoming and decidedly unstuffy and nights here are often longer than expected. (📞02-542-3333; Waldorf Astoria, 26-28 Agron St; ⏰6-11pm)

Gatsby's Cocktail Room

COCKTAIL BAR

27 🚇 MAP P80, D4

Renowned for its incredible cocktails in a city that loves its beer, Gatsby's Cocktail Room is intentionally hard to find, but that's part of the fun. To enter, pass through a nondescript white door at the end of the patio at Aroma Cafe and then another secret door disguised as a bookshelf. Ask the server about the day's specials or request your own mix: anything's possible here. (📞054-814-7143; www.facebook.com/Gatsby Jerusalem; 18 Hillel St; ⏰6pm-2am)

Hashchena Wine Bar

WINE BAR

28 🚇 MAP P80, E1

This cosy wine bar on the edge of Mahane Yehuda Market is a great place for an intimate drink, with seating inside and outside (the latter is the best for people watching). Hashchena (Hebrew for neighbourhood) is great for those wanting more than just a few quality wines to choose from: the list is extensive, as is the choice of local beers and speciality cocktails. (www.facebook.com/BarHashchena; 11 Beit Ya'akov St; ⏰7pm-2am; 🚊Mahane Yehuda)

Jabotinski

PUB

29 🚇 MAP P80, C4

Named after the Russian-born Zionist Ze'ev Jabotinsky (1880–1940), this pub and traveller hangout is one of a number of popular watering holes on Shim'on Ben Shatah St. The food is forgettable (ribs, burgers and the like), but the beer is cold, and there's plenty of streetside seating. (2 Shim'on Ben Shatah St; ⏰7pm-2am Sun-Fri, 1pm-late Sat; 📶; 🚊City Hall)

Entertainment

Hamiffal

ARTS CENTRE

30 ⭐ MAP P80, C6

Hamiffal (meaning 'the factory') is perfect for travellers looking to experience Jerusalem's alternative art and culture scene. Originally started by an art collective, Hamiffal now hosts Israeli and Palestinian concerts, lectures and courses and provides a space for people to drink, eat and jam together day and night. (www.facebook.com/hamiffal; 3 HaMa'aravim; ⏰noon-midnight

Sun-Thu, to 4pm Fri, 8pm-midnight Sat; City Hall)

HaMazkeka
LIVE MUSIC

31 ⭐ MAP P80, D4

HaMazkeka bustles late into weekend nights with people gathering for a drink and enjoying the sounds and sights of the city's independent artists. Check the venue's Facebook page (www.facebook.com/Mazkeka) to see what movies are being screened and which artists are performing throughout the week, or just stop by and watch the hip side of Jerusalem go by. (☎02-582-2090; www.mazkeka.com; 3 Shoshan St; ⏰8pm-4am; 🚊City Hall)

Time Elevator
THEATRE

32 ⭐ MAP P80, E6

Get jolted, sprinkled with water and blasted with sound effects on this cinematic journey through 3000 years of Jewish history. Chaim Topol – one-time star of *Fiddler on the Roof* – leads the audience through what is part museum, part theatre, and almost a carnival ride. It's especially recommended if you have children with you (over-fives only). Reservations required. There's disabled access. (☎02-624-8381; www.time-elevator.co.il; 6 Yitzhak Kariv Rd, Mamilla Mall; 54NIS; ⏰10am-9pm Sun-Thu, to 2pm Fri, noon-6pm Sat; 🚻; 🚊City Hall)

Machol Shalem Dance House
DANCE

33 ⭐ MAP P80, E3

The city's sole performing-arts space focused on fostering experimental dance, as well as other performing artists. (☎02-622-0907; www.macholshalem.org.il; 22 Shivtei Israel St, Russian Compound; ⏰office hours 9am-4pm)

Shopping

Halva Kingdom
FOOD

34 🔒 MAP P80, F1

Grinding sesame into paste since 1947, this irresistible stall is hard to miss thanks to its crown-shaped sign, huge wheels of halva and attendant proffering little samples of the flaky nougat. Once you've tasted it, you'll likely be hooked. Choose from flavours including rose, pistachio and chocolate, then await the sugar rush. (12 Etz HaChaim St, Mahane Yehuda Market; ⏰8am-sunset Sun-Thu, to 2pm Fri; 🚊Mahane Yehuda)

Artists' Colony
ARTS & CRAFTS

35 🔒 MAP P80, F8

One of the city's oldest streets, this cobblestone alleyway is lined with small artists' galleries and workshops producing jewellery, paintings, Judaica, sculptures, glassware and embroidery, among other crafts – you can often see the artisans at work. There's an annual arts and crafts festival here

Arman Darian Ceramic

in August. Check the website and contact particular workshops in advance if you want to be sure they'll be in. (Hutzot Hayotzer; www. artistscolony.co.il; Hutzot Hayotzer St; ☉10am-5pm Sun-Thu, to 2pm Fri; 🚌13, 18 & 38 to King David St)

Greenvurcel   GIFTS & SOUVENIRS

36 🚇 MAP P80, C4

Sleek, minimalist designs characterise the metalwork of versatile artist Yaakov Greenvurcel. His gleaming *challah* trays and dreidels are among the Judaica on offer; meanwhile, the jewellery – featuring Tahitian pearls, semi-precious gems and abstract designs – feels very contemporary. (☎02-622-1620; www.greenvurcel.

co.il; 27 Yo'el Salomon St; ☉10am-10pm Sun-Thu, to 2pm Fri, 1hr after Shabbat-11pm Sat; 🚌Jaffa Center)

Arman Darian Ceramic   CERAMICS

37 🚇 MAP P80, D5

Yerevan-born Arman Darian might be the best-known ceramicist in Israel, having installed his designs in many public buildings. Skilfully decorated ceramic vases, plates and tiles fill his workshop and boutique founded in 1986, as well as larger pieces such as tables topped with Armenian blue-and-white tiles. (☎02-623-4802; www. facebook.com/arman.darian.ceramic; 12 Shlomzion HaMalka St; ☉hours vary; 🚌City Hall)

Top Experience 📷

See a piece of the original Dead Sea Scrolls at the Israel Museum

Opened in 1965 and expanded in 2010, this extraordinary cultural institution is designed to resemble an Arab village. Exhibits include the Dead Sea Scrolls; a superb archaeological collection; rooms chock-full of Judaica and Jewish ethnographic displays; art galleries filled with works from Van Gogh, Monet and Renoir; and a sculpture garden replete with contemporary masterpieces.

www.imj.org.il

11 Ruppin Blvd, Museum Row

adult/student/child 54/39/27NIS

🕐 10am-5pm Sat-Mon, Wed & Thu, 4-9pm Tue, 10am-2pm Fri

Shrine of the Book & the Dead Sea Scrolls

One of the world's most important archaeological finds of the last century was the discovery of the Dead Sea Scrolls in 1947 in Qumran. The most important is the Great Isaiah Scroll, the largest (7.3m) and best preserved – it is reproduced in facsimile at the museum. The exhibit tells the story of the scrolls and the Essenes and displays some of the original documents. Each original piece is only displayed for several months at a time, before being placed back into containers for long-term preservation.

Archaeology Wing

Forming the most extensive collection of biblical and Holy Land archaeology in the world, the exhibits here are organised chronologically from prehistory to the Ottoman Empire. Displays include a group of 13th-century-BC human-shaped clay coffins found in Gaza; a 3rd-century mosaic floor from Nablus depicting events in the life of Achilles; and the 'House of David' Victory Stele, a fragmentary inscription from the First Temple period.

Fine Arts Wing

Highlights include the Impressionist and Post-Impressionist Gallery, which showcases work by Renoir, Pissarro, Degas, Sisley, Monet and Cézanne among others. The Modern Art Gallery has works by Schiele, Rothko, Motherwell, Pollock, Modigliani and Bacon, and Israeli art is well represented in the Israeli Art pavilion, with striking paintings by Reuven Rubin and Yosef Zaritsky.

★ **Top Tips**

○ Under 18s can enter for free on Tuesday and Saturday.

○ An animated kids film about the Dead Sea Scrolls is shown every hour on the half-hour.

○ The museum shop is one of the best in the city.

○ Download the museum app to use the free audio guide.

○ Gallery talks with various curators are held on Tuesday at 7pm and Wednesday at noon.

✕ **Take a Break**

The **Modern** (☏ 02-648-0862; www.modern.co.il; mains 65-120NIS; ⏱ 11.30am-5pm Sun-Thu, to late Tue; ✦) is a stylish, upscale cafe with outdoor patio seating.

★ **Getting There**

🚌 7, 9, 14, 32

Explore ⊛
German Colony & Southern Jerusalem

Upscale and cosmopolitan, the streets of Jerusalem's German Colony are lined with trees and chic cafes. Settled in the mid-19th century by German Templers, this multilingual area has a residual European flair. Together with several other southern Jerusalem neighbourhoods, the German Colony is popular with visitors seeking respite from downtown's roaring traffic and the frenetic Old City.

Begin to acquaint yourself with Jerusalem's south at Liberty Bell Park (p97) and Mishkenot Sha'anim – both are pleasant places to stroll and the latter provides fantastic views of the Old City. From there, the Begin Museum (p98) is close by – pop in for an interactive multimedia presentation on Menachem Begin, a central figure in the establishment of the state of Israel and its sixth Prime Minister. Finish the day by exploring a wide range of styles of Islamic art and a fabulous clock collection at the LA Mayer Museum for Islamic Art (p97).

Getting There & Around

Jerusalem's southern neighbourhoods are quite spread out: northern Rehavia is within a short walk of downtown, Yemin Moshe is close to the Old City and Baka is near Talpiot. Taxis are the most convenient way to get around.

🚍 Buses 7 and 34 travel to Emek Refa'im St from King George V St in downtown.

German Colony & Southern Jerusalem Map on p96

Pedestrians in the German Colony area EDDIE GERALD/GETTY IMAGES ©

Jerusalem German Colony & Southern Jerusalem

For reviews see

- Sights p97
- Eating p98
- Drinking p100
- Entertainment p101

Sights

LA Mayer Museum for Islamic Art

MUSEUM

1 ⊚ MAP P96, B3

The LA Mayer Museum, on Rehavia's southern fringe, exhibits ornate treasures from across the Islamic art world: 11th-century glassware and Mamluk pottery are worthy of attention, though the Iranian tile work steals the show. The museum serves as a useful primer on Islamic art's themes and development. Don't miss the museum's world-renowned collection of elaborately designed timepieces, including one made for Marie Antoinette. The story of how they were stolen and recovered is no less fascinating.

(☏02-566-1291; www.islamicart.
co.il; 2 HaPalmach St, Rehavia; adult/
student/child 40/30/20NIS; ⏱10am-
3pm Mon-Wed, to 7pm Thu, to 2pm Fri
& Sat; ➓13)

Liberty Bell Park

PARK

2 ⊚ MAP P96, E2

This grassy expanse covers parts of the Germany Colony and Talbieh neighbourhoods, and it's good for a picnic and a little bit of shade on hot days. Kids can enjoy a playground, and there's an area for roller skating and basketball courts and soccer fields. It's named after the replica of Philadelphia's original liberty bell in the centre of the park. (Gan Hapaamon)

Haas Promenade (p98)

Begin Museum
MUSEUM

3 MAP P96, E2

The life and times of Menachem Begin, a central figure in the establishment of the state of Israel and the country's sixth Prime Minister, is told through a lively hour-plus interactive multimedia presentation. Your experience is somewhat dependent on the quality of your guide, which can be hit or miss. Tours are offered in Hebrew, English, Russian, Arabic, French and Spanish. (☏02-565-2020; 6 Nakhon St, Yemin Moshe; adult/child 25/20NIS; ☉9am-4.30pm Sun, Mon, Wed & Thu, to 7pm Tue, to 12.30pm Fri)

Haas Promenade
VIEWPOINT

4 MAP P96, E4

The Haas Promenade offers cypress-framed views across Jerusalem: picture the Old City with tower blocks rising behind and village-speckled valleys rolling into the distance. Several walking paths allow for a variety of angles on this expansive view. Go in the late afternoon, when the picturesque ensemble is bathed in coppery light. (Talpiot)

St Andrew's Church
CHURCH

5 MAP P96, E2

Towering like a Highland castle, St Andrew's Church has been a small corner of Scotland ever since its first stone was laid in 1927. The so-called 'Scottish Church' was built in memory of the Scottish soldiers killed in action in the Holy Land during WWI. Scots continued to make use of the church during WWII, but these days a multitude of nationalities passes through, in particular to stop over at the excellent guesthouse. (☏02-673-2401; www.standrewsjerusalem.org; 1 David Remez St, German Colony; ☉church 9am-4pm Sun-Thu, to 1pm Fri)

Eating

Angelica
INTERNATIONAL $$$

6 MAP P96, D1

Sandstone arches and stone-framed windows establish a worldly tone at Angelica, but the menu is sheer invention. Appetisers marry a medley of cuisines: awaken your taste buds with aioli-drizzled fish shawarma served in a taco, or smoked almond and nectarine salad doused in champagne vinaigrette. Mains borrow bistro classics from across Europe, such as goose breast with beans, hanger steak, and mushroom ravioli. (☏02-623-0056; www.angelicarest.com; 4 George Washington St, Yemin Moshe; mains 92-158NIS; ☉12.30-10.30pm Sun-Thu, 8.30-11pm Sat)

Lev Smadar
ITALIAN $$$

7 MAP P96, D4

Carved out of a British hanger, this space was saved by the community and renovated into an intimate and sophisticated restaurant with a one-screen cinema attached.

Red chequered tablecloths and candles set the scene for the menu of refined and artfully prepared pasta dishes like bucatini with red wine, date honey, mushrooms and pears. The menu is complemented by a selection of fine Israeli and European wines. (☑02-566-0954; www.facebook.com/cafesmadar; 4 Lloyd George St, German Colony; mains 56-92NIS; ⊗4pm-midnight Sun-Thu, from noon Fri, from 9am Sat; 🛜)

First Station   FOOD HALL $$

8 ❌ MAP P96, E3

This dining and entertainment complex, housed in a handsome 19th-century railway station, is an atmospheric place for a sit-down meal or a few beers. There are boutiques, cafes and an ice cream stand, plus more than a dozen restaurants, including kosher steak (Bread & Meat), Italian (Fiori) and Asian (Station 9) joints. It's popular with families during the day and gets lively after dark. (☑02 653-5239; www.firststation.co.il; 4 David Remez St, German Colony; mains from 55NIS; ⊗7am-late; ✍)

From Gaza to Berlin   ISRAELI $$

9 ❌ MAP P96, B2

Just the basics, in terms of decor and menu, but the talafel and hummus are considered the best in the neighbourhood. The name refers to the restaurant's road intersection location. (1 HaRav Haim Berlin St, Rehavia; mains 35NIS; ⊗10am-10pm Sun-Thu, 9am-4pm Fri)

Marzipan Bakery & Coffee Shop   BAKERY $$

10 ❌ MAP P96, C4

This bakery is so synonymous with its speciality chocolate *rugelach* (rolled-up pastries with variety of fillings) that some refer to them as 'marzipan'. This spot also turns out cinnamon buns, *challah*, Moroccan cookies, Syrian pastries, cream puffs, *bourekas* (flaky pastries) and croissants. There's a full-service cafe with coffee and sandwiches as well. (www.marzipanbakery.com; 5 Rachel Imenu St, Emek Refaim; mains 38NIS; ⊗8am-6pm Sun-Thu, 7am-4pm Sun)

Abu Shukri   ISRAELI $$

11 ❌ MAP P96, E3

Anchoring the southern end of the First Station complex's restaurant row, this imitator of the Old City original does a close approximation in terms of the quality of the food. Great variety of salads, hummus dishes, plus grilled meats. (First Station, 4 David Remez St, German Colony; mains 32-68NIS; ⊗10am-11pm; 🛜)

P2   ITALIAN $$

12 ❌ MAP P96, D1

This small local favourite with front patio seating does excellent wood-fired, thin-crust pizzas and house-made pastas. Because of its proximity to several large hotels, a fair number of tourists can wander in. (☑02-563-5555;

First Station (p99)

36 Karen HaYesod St, Talbieh; mains 55NIS; ☺noon-midnight)

Drinking

Talbiye
WINE BAR

13 🚇 MAP P96, C2

Israeli and international wines flow freely at this bohemian-feel bar, whose antique furnishings and location underneath the **Jerusalem Theatre** (Jerusalem Centre for the Performing Arts; 📞02-560-5755; www.jerusalem-theatre.co.il; ☺box office 9.30am-7.30pm Sun-Thu, to 1pm Fri) pull a worldly, moneyed crowd of revellers and literati. (📞02-581-1927; www.talbiye.com; 5 Chopin St, Talbiyeh; ☺9.30am-4.30pm & 5pm-midnight)

Carousela
CAFE

14 🚇 MAP P96, A2

Just off relatively bustling Azza St, this funky spot is where locals go for strong coffee and creative cocktails. Offers outdoor seating and occasional live music and other cultural events. (1 Binyamin mi-Tudela, Rechavia; ☺8am-midnight Sat-Thu, to 3pm Fri)

HaSadna
COCKTAIL BAR

15 🚇 MAP P96, E3

The owners of much-loved Machneyuda (p84) recreated their magic here, combining style with substance, in this former railroad warehouse redesigned as a classy and chic space with a large three-sided bar. Indulge with creative cocktails, a large wine selection and shots of arak. (The Culinary Workshop; ☑02-567-2265; www.hasadna.rest-e.co.il; 28 Hebron Rd, Giva't Hananya; ⊘6.30pm-late Sun-Thu, noon-3pm & 6pm-late Fri, 12.30pm-late Sat)

Coffee Mill

CAFE

16 MAP P96, D4

Bustling and bookish Coffee Mill draws a multilingual crowd to sip lattes between walls lined with coffee beans and covers of the *New Yorker*. Coffee Mill also serves decent breakfasts, including omelettes, cream cheese–slathered bagels, flapjacks and gluten-free cookies. (☑02-566-1665; 23 Emek Refaim St, German Colony; ⊘7.30am-11pm Sun-Thu, to 3pm Fri; 🚌4, 18, 21)

Entertainment

Cinematheque

CINEMA

17 😊 MAP P96, E2

The Jerusalem Cinematheque, with its quality foreign films and mini festivals on diverse themes such as gay cinema and China on the silver screen, is a hangout for true movie connoisseurs. It's a favoured haunt of secular, left-leaning Jerusalemites and the home of the respected **Jerusalem Film Festival** (www.jff.org. il; ⊘end Jul-early Aug). (☑02-565-4333; www.jer-cin.org.il; Sultan's Pool, 11 Hebron Rd, Yemin Moshe; tickets 39NIS; 🚌34, 7, 8, 18, 71, 72, 74, 77, 38)

Yellow Submarine

LIVE MUSIC

18 😊 MAP P96, B4

Does Middle Eastern dance music or Balkan pop sound like your jam? How about soft jazz, Jewish spiritual songs or stand-up comedy? An impressively diverse program of musical and spoken-word talent takes the stage at Yellow Submarine; browse the website for upcoming events. (☑02-679-4040, www.yellowsubmarine.org.il; 13 Herkevim St, Talpiot)

UZIEL עוזיאל

Top Experience 📷

Pay your respects at Yad Vashem's Holocaust memorials

Ponder tragedy, evil, human resilience and reconciliation at Yad Vashem, a memorial to the six million Jews who died during the Holocaust. The museum lays out the history of European anti-Semitism, tethering it to each country's and region's particularities. Labyrinthine corridors with multimedia exhibitions end with a symbolic coming into light.

www.yadvashem.org

Hazikaron St, Har Hazikaron

admission free

🕑 8.30am-5pm Sun-Wed, to 8pm Thu, to 2pm Fri

🚌 13, 16, 17, 20, 21, 23, 26, 27, 33, 🚊 Mt Herzl

Design

The Moshe Safdie–designed museum, which replaced an older version in 2005, is the centre-piece of Yad Vashem. To give you a sense of the complexity and density of its galleries, consider that the audio guide (35NIS; in eight languages) has seven hours of content. When you throw in the morally unsettling nature of the subject, most people can only visit for several hours before exhaustion kicks in.

The building itself is a prism-shaped concrete underground bunker-like space divided by a series of symbolic cuts (with their own displays) that separates galleries on either side of the gently sloping floor. The first cut documents the beginnings of Nazi ideology with book burning in 1933. Throughout, as the consequences of anti-Semitism become more barbaric, the museum weaves in the political question, namely 'where is the rest of the world?'

Text & Visuals

The museum's extraordinary power is generated by displays pairing mundane-seeming official documents with visual representations of what they actually called for: the destruction of European Jewry. There's a blown-up, wall-sized chart, part of the infamous 1942 Wannsee Conference where high-ranking Nazi officials discussed the 'Final Solution', listing the number of remaining Jews in each country. Also on show is Heinrich Himmler's typed order to 'resettle' Jewish ghetto populations to death camps. Next comes a model of the Birkenau gas chamber and underground crematorium (part of the Auschwitz 'labour camp' complex) and photos of piles of dead bodies and skeletal survivors when the camp was liberated at the end of the war.

Equally troubling are the films commissioned by the Nazi Ministry of Public Enlightenment and Propaganda in 1939 with the express

★ **Getting There**

It's a 10-minute walk from the Mt Herzl stop of the light-rail line to the museum. Free buses make the trip every 20 minutes.

★ **Top Tips**

o Head to the Visual Center (9am to 5pm) for screenings of documentaries, news clips and feature films – anything related to the Holocaust.

o The website has an excellent virtual tour of the museum if you want to 'visit' the galleries you missed.

o Kids under 12 are discouraged from visiting.

✕ **Take a Break**

The basement cafeteria has two options: one, a basic run-of-the-mill with simple sandwiches, salads and pastries. The other offers pricier, fuller meals, including daily meat and vegetarian specialities, plus a good salad bar.

mission of portraying Jews as less than human. In the museum, small screens with subtitles show several. One of these, called *Jued Suss* (Jew Suss), shows the story of a Jewish banker who is executed after raping the Aryan heroine, and was required viewing for members of the SS, a Nazi paramilitary organisation.

Housed in its own building, the **Museum of Holocaust Art** is a powerful reminder of the urge of the human spirit to create even in the face of terrible suffering. Many of the paintings and drawings on display were created by Jewish artists in ghettos or while they were on the run hiding from Nazi authorities; many of the artists featured were subsequently killed, including Bruno Schulz, a prominent Polish-Jewish writer, and Charlotte Salomon, a German-Jewish painter.

The powerful **testimony of Holocaust survivors**, the documenting of which is one of Yad Vashem's more important missions, can be seen in several places in the museum and the complete archive is available for viewing in the Visual Center.

Memorials

Many people don't have the time or energy to wander the grounds after visiting the Holocaust History Museum, but it's well worth the effort. Close to the visitors centre is the wrenching and sombre **Children's Memorial**, dedicated to the 1.5 million Jewish children who died in the Holocaust. The underground memorial contains a solitary flame reflected infinitely by hundreds of mirrors. Recorded voices read the names of children who perished. Close by, **Warsaw Ghetto Square** contains an imposing red-brick memorial to the fierce resistance of fighters in the Warsaw Ghetto Uprising of 1943.

In the **Hall of Remembrance** on the ground level, an eternal flame burns near a crypt containing the ashes of victims brought from the death camps; the floor is engraved with the names of 22 of the most infamous Nazi extermination camps.

Behind the hall are a number of other memorials, including the **Cattle Car Memorial**, one of the original train cars used to transport Jews from the ghettos to the camps. Also here is the **Garden of the Righteous Among the Nations**, established in honour of the thousands of non-Jews who risked their lives to rescue Jews during the Holocaust. Others include the **Pillar of Heroism**, a column dedicated to Jewish resistance fighters; the **Family Plaza sculpture** marking the families destroyed; the **Monument to Jewish Soldiers & Partisans**, six massive arrow-shaped stones facing one another; and the **Partisans' Panorama** with a striking life-sized sculpture of a tree symbolising the forest's importance as a refuge for the fighters.

Worth a Trip 🔭
Float in the Dead Sea

The lowest place on earth, the Dead Sea (431m below sea level) brings together breathtaking natural beauty, compelling ancient history and modern mineral spas that soothe and pamper every fibre of your body. The jagged bluffs of the Judaean Desert, cleft by dry canyons that turn into raging tan-coloured torrents after a cloudburst, rise from the cobalt blue waters of the Dead Sea, heavy with salt and oily with minerals.

From Jerusalem Egged buses 444 and 486 (34NIS, one hour to Ein Gedi, about hourly 6.30am to 4.45pm Sunday to Thursday, until 2pm Friday, at least one Saturday night)

From Tel Aviv Egged bus 421 (48.40NIS, 2 hours to Ein Bokek, three daily Sunday to Thursday, one on Friday)

Ein Bokek

Sandwiched between the turquoise waters of the southern Dead Sea and a dramatic tan bluff, Ein Bokek's strip of luxury hotels is the region's main tourist zone. It has the area's nicest free beaches and is the Dead Sea's main centre for treating ailments such as psoriasis, arthritis and respiratory conditions with naturally occurring minerals and compounds.

Unlike the beaches along the lake's northern basin, Ein Bokek fronts evaporation pools (kept full by Dead Sea Works pumps) rather than the open sea. Its lakeshore is not receding and sinkholes are not a problem here.

Day Spas

Almost every Ein Bokek hotel boasts a spa with swimming pools, saunas, mineral baths, a long menu of health treatments and an army of predominantly Russian therapists. Most places charge nonguests 140NIS to 220NIS to use their facilities for the day, including beach chairs but not including special treatments. Some deals include lunch.

Healing Properties

The waters of the Dead Sea contain 20 times as much bromine, 15 times more magnesium and 10 times as much iodine as the ocean. Bromine, a component of many sedatives, relaxes the nerves; magnesium counteracts skin allergies and clears the bronchial passages; and iodine has a beneficial effect on certain glandular functions – or so it's claimed.

The Dead Sea's extremely dense air – the area has the world's highest barometric pressure – has 10% more oxygen than sea-level air. Other properties, especially good for people with breathing problems, include low rainfall, pollution and humidity; high temperatures and pollen-free air.

★ Top Tips

o Don't shave the day before you swim; nicks and cuts are likely to call attention to themselves.

o Wear waterproof sandals to protect your feet from the sun-scorched sand and, in some places, from sharp stones, both on shore and in the water.

o It's always a good idea to put on sunscreen, even if ultra-low-elevation air naturally filters the sun's harmful ultra-violet rays, making it much harder to get sunburnt than at sea level, despite scorching temperatures.

o Do not under any circumstances dunk your head! If water gets in your eyes, calmly get out of the water and ask someone to help you rinse your eyes under a shower or tap (the Ein Bokek beaches have special eyewash stations).

o Drink *lots* of water – the Dead Sea is so saturated with minerals that it will suck out your body's fluids like a thousand leeches.

Tel Aviv Neighbourhoods

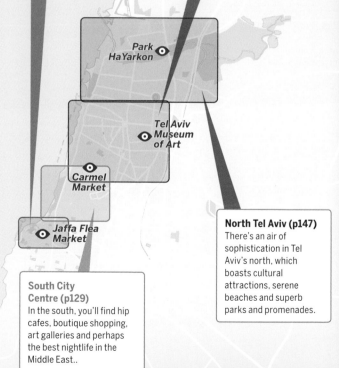

Jaffa (Yafo; p159)
A wander through Jaffa's ancient atmospheric streets reveals bohemian bars, charming cafes and a legendary flea market.

Tel Aviv City Centre (p111)
Tel Aviv's heart is home to top museums, high-end shops, world-class eateries and the city's most buzzing beaches.

Park HaYarkon

Tel Aviv Museum of Art

Carmel Market

Jaffa Flea Market

North Tel Aviv (p147)
There's an air of sophistication in Tel Aviv's north, which boasts cultural attractions, serene beaches and superb parks and promenades.

South City Centre (p129)
In the south, you'll find hip cafes, boutique shopping, art galleries and perhaps the best nightlife in the Middle East..

Explore
Tel Aviv

Modern, vibrant and cosmopolitan, Tel Aviv has an enterprising creative landscape. Its after-dark culture – centred on jovial rooftop rounds, live music at neighbourhood dives and international DJs spinning bumping beats at underground clubs – leaves no shortage of options for a party fit to your tastes. A strip of shimmering seashore, stretching 14km along the Mediterranean coast, is the city's crowning glory.

Explore
City Centre

The city centre (also known as Merkaz ha-Ir or Lev ha-Ir) is Tel Aviv's vibrant heart. Home to top-notch beaches, museums and eateries, it encompasses the arts precinct around Habima Sq; a stretch of the city's favourite promenade, Rothschild Blvd; shopping hubs Dizengoff Centre and Sarona; retail and cafe strips along Dizengoff, Allenby and King George Sts; and the central beaches, Gordon, Frishman and Bograshov.

For easy access to the city centre's sights, base yourself near Dizengoff Sq, where you'll find loads of bars and cafes stretching north along Dizengoff St. Tel Aviv's central beaches, Gordon, Frishman and Bograshov, are within easy walking distance. To the east is Rabin Square (p116), the largest public square in the city, and the Tel Aviv Museum of Art (p112), which is home to the country's largest collections of international and Israeli art. A few blocks south you'll find Sarona (p124), Tel Aviv's swankiest market – explore its shops, galleries and street-food stalls, all set in a complex of restored German Templer houses.

Getting There & Around

Right in the thick of it all, the city centre is one of Tel Aviv's easiest and most pleasant neighbourhoods for biking – you'll find designated paths along Ben Gurion, Ben Tsiyon, Rothschild and Chen Boulevards. Taxis, buses and sheruts are also plentiful.

🚌 Route number 5 runs from Central Station (ground floor) along many city centre streets, including Allenby St up to Rothschild Blvd, Dizengoff St, and over to Ibn Gabriol St.

🚕 Sheruts take the same route as bus 5; operate on Shabbat.

City Centre Map on p114

Tel Aviv Museum of Art (p112), designed by Preston Scott Cohen

Top Experience 📷

Catch a film or show at the Tel Aviv Museum of Art

Set partly within a striking structure that's an architectural wonder itself, this three-venue museum is home to the country's most comprehensive modern, contemporary and Israeli art collections. It also houses an impressive variety of works by renowned 16th- to 19th-century masters, photography displays, and a regular rotation of diverse temporary exhibitions.

◉ MAP P114, G3

www.tamuseum.org.il

27 Shaul HaMelech Blvd

adult/student/child under 15yr 50/40NIS/free

⏱10am-6pm Mon-Wed & Sat, to 9pm Tue & Thu, to 2pm Fri

Homegrown Artists

Here, among the ranks of renowned inter-national artists, you'll find the country's homegrown greats. This museum houses the world's most comprehensive collection of works by artists who have heritage here, and exhibitions trace the history and sociopolitical themes from the prestate era to contemporary times.

Notable works include the *Yemenite Boy* (c 1914) sculpture by Ze'ev Raban (1890–1970), created after he arrived in the state and joined the staff of the Bezalel School of Art. It was here that Raban first encountered Yemenite Jews, who worked in the school's craft departments and sat as models for the artist's depictions of biblical figures – indigenous character studies, primarily of Yemenites, would soon form the body of Raban's sculptural work.

One of the country's most prominent artists, Nahum Gutman's (1898–1980) modernist *Resting at Noon* (1926) painting is an example of his deference to Arabs as models. This was an attitude held by several local artists in the 1920s, who believed Arabs embodied a vitality that defined the true essence of the Middle East – juxtaposing the stereotypical likeness of Diaspora Jews.

★ Top Tips

o Free English-speaking tours of the museum's Israeli and Impressionist-to-mid-20th century collections are con-ducted Thursdays at noon.

o The museum stays open until 9pm on Tuesdays and Thurs-days, making it a great end to a day of sightseeing around the city centre.

o The museum regu-larly hosts events like film screenings, dance shows and music festivals – check the calendar on the website to plan ahead.

✕ Take a Break

Head to the Pastel brasserie in the Herta and Paul Amir Building, or the Din-ing Hall of the Israeli Opera (p122) next door.

If you're up for a short walk, great restaurants and food stalls in Sarona (p124) are just 10 minutes away.

★ Getting There

🚌 9, 18, 28, 70, 90, 111

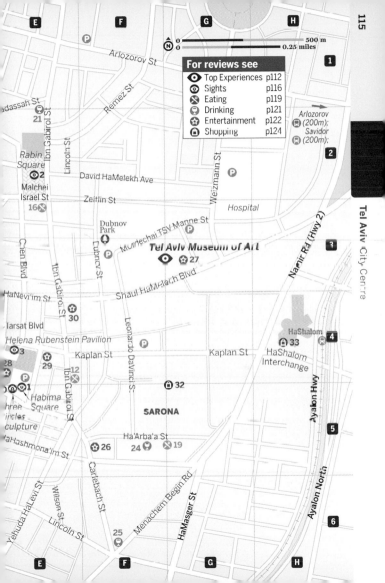

Tel Aviv City Centre

E **F** **G** **H**

Arlozorov St

N 0
0
0.25 miles
500 m

1

For reviews see

⊙	Top Experiences	p112
⊙	Sights	p116
✕	Eating	p119
⊟	Drinking	p121
☆	Entertainment	p122
🛍	Shopping	p124

Arlozorov
(200m);
Savidor
(200m);

2

Remez St

Weizmann St

adassah St

21

Ibn Gabirol St

Lincoln St

*Rabin
Square*

⊙2

Malchei
Israel St

16✕

David HaMelekh Ave

Zeitlin St

Hospital

Namir Rd (Hwy 2)

Chen Blvd

*Dubnov
Park*

Dubnov St

Mordechai TSV Manne St

Tel Aviv Museum of Art

⊙ ☆27

3

HaNevi'im St

Ibn Gabirol St

☆30

Shaul HaMelech Blvd

Jarsat Blvd

Helena Rubenstein Pavilion

⊙3

28

☆

☆29

Kaplan St

Leonardo Davinci St

Kaplan St

HaShalom

🛍33

HaShalom
Interchange

4

🅟

⊙⊙1

hree

ircles

culpture

Ibn Gabirol St

12

*Habima
Square*

🛍32

SARONA

HaShalom

Ayalon Hwy

Ha'Arba'a St

5

aHashmona'im St

☆26

24⊟

✕19

Yehuda Halevi St

Wilson St

Lincoln St

Carlebach St

25
⊟

Menachem Begin Rd

HaMasger St

Ayalon North

6

E **F** **G** **H**

Sights

Habima Square   SQUARE

1 ◎ MAP P114, E5

Home to a handful of Tel Aviv's top cultural institutions – Helena Rubenstein Pavilion, Charles Bronfman Auditorium (p123) and Habima National Theatre (p123) – this expansive plaza is a great place to stop and bask in the bright glow of the city's Bauhaus structures. At first approach, the *Three Circles* Sculpture (p119) dominates the landscape, but a stroll around reveals a peaceful sunken garden and reflecting pool that adds a little colour and movement to all those clean lines. (Tarsat Blvd 2)

Rabin Square   SQUARE

2 ◎ MAP P114, E2

The biggest public square in the city, this huge expanse of paving stones was repaved and upgraded in recent years. It has an ecological pond filled with lotus flowers and koi, a fountain that's lit up at night and some cool cafes around the perimeter. On the northern edge towers City Hall, which looks like a 1960s communist-style block (though not when it's lit up with laser beams).

Helena Rubenstein Pavilion   GALLERY

3 ◎ MAP P114, E4

Endowed by the cosmetics entrepreneur of the same name, this contemporary-art space is an annex of the Tel Aviv Museum of Art (p112). There's a permanent collection of decorative arts on the top floor, but the main draw is the temporary exhibition space downstairs, which showcases work by both Israeli and international artists – it's a good place to feel the pulse of Tel Aviv's ever-evolving artistic scene. (📞03-528-7196; www. tamuseum.org.il/helena-rubinstein-pavilion; 6 Tarsat Blvd; admission free; ⏰10am-6pm Mon, Wed & Sat, to 9pm Tue & Thu, to 2pm Fri)

Ben-Gurion House   MUSEUM

4 ◎ MAP P114, B1

Built between 1930 and 1931, this modest house on the way to the seafront was the Tel Aviv home of David Ben-Gurion, Israel's first prime minister. Built in a workers' neighbourhood, it is maintained more or less as it was left on the great man's death. Downstairs visitors can view photographs of Ben-Gurion meeting famous figures such as Nixon, Kennedy and Einstein, while upstairs is home to the former PM's library and thousands of books in different languages. (📞03-522-1010; www.bg-house.org; 17 Ben-Gurion Blvd; admission free; ⏰8am-3pm Sun & Tue-Thu, to 5pm Mon, to 1pm Fri, 11am-2pm Sat)

Rubin Museum   GALLERY

5 ◎ MAP P114, B5

Sometimes referred to as the 'Gauguin of Palestine' but more reminiscent of Matisse, Romanian-born Reuven Rubin (1893–1974) immigrated to Palestine in 1923 and painted wonderful landscapes and scenes of local life in his adopted home. Set in his former house, the gallery hosts a number of scenes of Jaffa and plenty of portraits, providing a fascinating account of Jewish immigration and the early years of Israel. (🖉 03-525-5961; www.rubinmuseum.org.il; 14 Bialik St; adult/child 20NIS/free; 🕑10am-3pm Mon, Thu & Fri, to 8pm Tue, 11am-2pm Sat & Sun)

custom-made furniture, a vivid colour scheme and ceramic tiles representing the Twelve Tribes of Israel, the Star of David and the signs of the zodiac. Bialik's private library, study and bedroom are preserved upstairs, and there's an archive of his papers in the basement. (🖉 03-525-3403; https://beithair.org/en/bialik_house; 22 Bialik St; adult/student & child 20/10NIS, incl Beit Ha'ir adult 30NIS; 🕑11am-5pm Mon-Thu, 10am-2pm Fri & Sat)

Bialik Museum   MUSEUM

6 ◉ MAP P114, C4

Israel's national poet Chaim Nachman Bialik lived in this handsome 1920s villa, which is designed in the style of the Arts and Crafts movement. Its richly decorated downstairs interiors include

Beit Ha'ir   CULTURAL CENTRE

7 ◉ MAP P114, C4

Located in a cul de sac at the end of Bialik St, which is full of significant Bauhaus-style buildings, this cultural centre comprises two galleries where temporary exhibitions are held, as well as a permanent

Bialik Museum

exhibition of historical photographs and documents about the city. The building, which dates from 1925, was used as Tel Aviv's city hall until 1965 and visitors can see a reconstruction of the office once used by Meir Dizengoff. (Town House; 📞03-724-0311; http://beithair.org; 27 Bialik St; adult/student & child 20/10NIS, incl Bialik Museum adult 30NIS; 🕘9am-5pm Mon-Thu, 10am-2pm Fri & Sat)

Jabotinsky Institute MUSEUM

8 ◉ MAP P114, D4

Political history buffs will enjoy this research organisation's small museum that presents the history and activities of the Etzel (Irgun), an underground militia founded by Ze'ev Jabotinsky in 1931. Exhibits concentrate on Jabotinsky's

political, literary and journalistic activities, and also document the creation of the Jewish Legion (five battalions of Jewish volunteers who served in the British army during WWI). (📞03-528-6523; www.jabotinsky.org; 38 King George St; admission free; 🕘8am-4pm Sun-Thu)

Gan Meir Park PARK

9 ◉ MAP P114, C4

To escape the city pace, head to Gan Meir Park, on the western side of King George St, where dog walkers release their four-legged friends in a specially designated dog run, and parents do the same to their two-legged charges at the playground. There's plenty of tree-shaded space and picnic benches for some lunchtime lounging.

Three Circles Sculpture and Habima National Theatre (p123)

Three Circles Sculpture

SCULPTURE

10 ⊙ MAP P114, E5

An icon on Habima Sq, this looming, minimalist steel sculpture by Menashe Kadishman (1932–2015) was constructed from 1967 to 1976 to address the economic instability that plagued the country during those years. Composed of – you guessed it – three circles stacked 15m high at a slight diagonal, it was the subject of controversy in 2015 when the mayor put a hot-pink bra on two of them in an effort to raise breast cancer awareness. (Hitromemut (Uprise); Habima Sq)

Eating

Miznon

ISRAELI $

11 ✖ MAP P114, C5

The vibe here is bustling, the prices are (very) reasonable and the staff is friendly and full of energy. And let's not forget the most important thing: the food is exceptionally delicious. Huge pitas stuffed with your choice of veggies, chicken, offal or meat await, as do fish and chips or roasted spiced yam and cauliflower (yum!). (📞03-631-7688; www.miznon.com; 30 King George St; pitas 25-49NIS; ⊙noon-1am Sun-Thu, to 3pm Fri, from 7pm Sat; 🖋)

Ha'achim

ISRAELI $$

12 ✖ MAP P114, E4

Ha'achim, meaning 'the brothers' in Hebrew, has a distinctly Mediterranean menu of hummus, *labneh* (thick yoghurt flavoured with garlic and sometimes with mint), tahini, olives and complimentary pita breads with olive oil. Much more than a hummus joint, there are chef specials and grilled meat and fish. (📞03-691-7171; www.haachim.co.il; 12 Ibn Gabirol St; mains 27-89NIS; ⊙noon-midnight; 🖋)

La Shuk

MEDITERRANEAN $$$

13 ✖ MAP P114, C3

Lively La Shuk (the market) is in a fab location on the corner of Dizengoff Sq, with a busy but pleasant patio to watch the Tel Aviv chaos go by. Great for brunches or night-time meals, the kitchen serves up a wide mixture of 'market' cuisine, such as large shared salads, pasta, seafood, kebabs and more. (📞03-603-3117; www.la-shuk.co.il; 92 Dizengoff St; brunch from 49NIS, mains from 73NIS; ⊙5pm-midnight Sun-Thu, noon-1am Fri & Sat, 🖋)

Thai House

THAI $$$

14 ✖ MAP P114, B3

Bamboo-laden walls, ceilings and furnishings whisk diners from Tel Aviv's concrete frenzy to a Southeast Asian beach scene. Home to the first and, some say, best Thai food in the city, quality and portions are top notch. The extensive menu caters to all dietary considerations and the exotic cocktails go down easy to quench the burn. (📞03-517-8568; www.thai-house.co.il; 8 Bograshov St; mains 74-148NIS; ⊙noon-5pm & 6-11pm; 🖋)

Sarona (p124)

Tamara   ICE CREAM $

15 ✖ MAP P114, C2

Indulgent but delicious, Tamara, near Gordon Beach, is the best frozen yoghurt in town (and there are a few to contend with). Enjoy your cup plain or choose from a range of toppings. Besides yoghurt, it also sells refreshing fruit tapioca and *paletas* (Mexican fruit ice blocks). Kids can sit on swings while adults queue for their yoghurt. (96 Ben Yehuda St; small/ medium/large cup 26/32/38NIS; ⊙10am-midnight)

Savta   SANDWICHES $

16 ✖ MAP P114, E3

Just south of Rabin Sq, this cheery, chequerboard-floored kiosk slings hearty sub-style sandwiches with

quality ingredients. Hip, friendly workers craft the deliciously straightforward creations with a care that'd surely make *savta* ('grandmother' in Hebrew) proud. It's veggie friendly, but carnivores shouldn't miss the Sleazy, which features grilled salami, pastrami and lamb bacon paired with gooey Gouda and caramelised onions. (📞03-573-7479; www.ilovesavta.com; 65 Ibn Gabirol St; sandwiches 17-49NIS; ⊙10am-11pm Sun-Thu, to 4pm Fri, 6-11pm Sat; ✎)

HaKosem   MIDDLE EASTERN $

17 ✖ MAP P114, D3

One of the friendliest falafel stalls in town, HaKosem (the Magician) is a popular snack stop on the corner of King George St. Aside from its trademark green, fried chickpea balls in pita, it also offers *sabich* (egg, aubergine and salad in pita) and shawarma (meat sliced off a spit and stuffed in a bread wrap with tomatoes and garnish). (☎03-525-2033; www.falafelhakosem.com; 1 Shlomo HaMelech St; falafel from 12NIS; ⏲9.30am-midnight Sun-Thu, 9am-4.30pm Fri; ✐)

Falafel Gabai   MIDDLE EASTERN $

18 ✖ MAP P114, B3

In a city where every falafel stall claims to be the best, Gabai is a strong contender for the title. Like most stalls, its crispy balls of falafel come with as much salad, pickles and tahina sauce as you can squeeze in a pita bread. It also serves a fine shakshuka and schnitzel. (25 Bograshov St; falafel 19NIS; ⏲11am-10.30pm Sun-Thu, to 2pm Fri; ✐)

416   VEGAN $$

19 ✖ MAP P114, G5

This is a vegan restaurant with attitude. The concept is simple: take comfort food favourites and serve them with all the trimmings (without harming any animals). Expect dishes like mushroom schnitzel baguette, vegan shawarma and even juicy seitan steak, served in a pan with potatoes and onions. This guilt-free indulgence makes 416 popular with vegans and non-vegans alike. (☎03-775-5060; https://416.co.il; 16 Ha'Arba'a St; mains 52-68NIS; ⏲noon-11pm; ✐)

Goocha   SEAFOOD $$

20 ✖ MAP P114, C1

Not to be confused with its newer sibling restaurant, the Goocha Diner on Ibn Gabirol St, Goocha is the original and better of the two. Locals and tourists flock here for dishes such as *moules and frites*, shrimp burger and seafood risotto. Thanks to its fab spot on the corner of Ben-Gurion Ave, it's always packed and advance booking is advised. (☎03-522-2886; www.goocha.co.il; 171 Dizengoff St; mains 65-109NIS; ⏲noon-1am; 🛜)

Drinking

Kanta   ROOFTOP BAR

21 🍷 MAP P114, E2

On the rooftop of the Gan Ha'Ir (City Garden) shopping mall, trendy Kanta has one of the finest outdoor terraces in Tel Aviv. Surrounded by plants and lit up at night, this urban garden is great for summer, but it also shines in winter, when it gets enclosed and the outdoor heaters take up residence. (http://kanta.co.il; 71 Ibn Gabirol; ⏲8pm-3am; 🛜)

Spicehaus   COCKTAIL BAR

22 🍷 MAP P114, C2

If you're suffering from a case of craft cocktail thirst, come sip potions with a pharmaceutical flair at this one-of-a-kind watering hole, where antique medical devices and vintage ephemera create a unique apothecary vibe.

Mixologists even dress the part and select spirits – some made for sharing – are served in quirky receptacles like beakers or syringes. (☏03-518-6217; www.facebook.com/SSpicehaus.tv; 117 Dizengoff St; ◷6pm-3am Sun-Thu, from 1pm Fri, from 4pm Sat)

Beer Garden BAR

23 MAP P114, C3

Buzzing and always busy, Beer Garden attracts crowds of Tel Avivians to its corner of Dizengoff Sq. Though it may look like there's plenty of room on the pavement outside and inside around its bar, it's still advisable to reserve a table. The menu includes lots of German and Belgian beers, plus Oktoberfest-style sausages. (☏054-527-4512; 2 Raines St; ◷6.30pm-2am)

Porter & Sons PUB

24 MAP P114, F5

This big German-inspired pub located on the main street behind the Sarona market (p124) is best known for offering more than 50 kinds of beer, both international and Israeli boutique brews, on tap. Popular with the business crowd, it offers beer tastings, comfortable booths and traditional pub food such as bratwurst, burgers and fish and chips. (☏03-624-4355; www.porter.co.il; 14 Ha'Arba'a St; ◷5pm-midnight Sun-Tue & Sat, noon-midnight Wed, noon-1am Thu & Fri)

Beit Maariv CLUB

25 MAP P114, F6

It's all about the sound at Beit Maariv, one of the best clubs in the city's underground dance scene. A total astral experience with lasers and huge speakers, this club is housed in the building that was once used for the Israeli newspaper *Maariv*. It's now home to some of the top local and international house DJs. (www.facebook.com/BeitMaariv; 51 Menachem Begin Rd; entry 70-100NIS; ◷11.30pm-late Thu-Sat; ☐26, 89, 189)

Entertainment

Cinematheque CINEMA

26 MAP P114, F5

The flagship in a chain of Israeli cinemas, this branch draws a cultured local crowd for its screenings of classic, retro, foreign, avant-garde and experimental films. It often holds film festivals, such as DocAviv. (☏03-606-0800; www.cinema.co.il/english; 1 Ha'Arba'a St; from 30NIS; ◷10am-midnight Sun-Fri, from 11am Sat)

Israeli Opera OPERA

27 MAP P114, G3

The city's major opera house is also home to the Israel Ballet. It's located in the complex next to the Tel Aviv Museum of Art and Cameri Theatre. (☏03-692-7777; www.israel-opera.co.il; 19 Shaul HaMelech Blvd)

Habima National Theatre THEATRE

28 ⭐ MAP P114, E4

Home to Israel's national theatre company, Habima stages weekly performances in its restored, modern dome-shaped building. Most have simultaneous subtitles in English. (☎03-629-5555; www. habima.co.il; 2 Tarsat Blvd, Habima Sq)

Charles Bronfman Auditorium CLASSICAL MUSIC

29 ⭐ MAP P114, E4

Home to the Israel Philharmonic Orchestra, the Charles Bronfman Auditorium plays host to world-class classical music performances several times a week. Look out for the occasional children's performances with sto-

ries (from 60NIS per child, free for adults). (☎03-621-1777; www. ipo.co.il; Habima Sq)

Tzavta THEATRE

30 ⭐ MAP P114, E4

This 'progressive' club-theatre, founded by the far-left HaShomer HaTzair youth movement, has pop and folk Israeli music concerts, as well as Hebrew-language theatre and comedy. Most performances held here are in Hebrew, though it occasionally holds English plays. (☎03-695-0156; www.tzavta.co.il; 30 Ibn Gabirol St)

Ozen Bar LIVE MUSIC

31 ⭐ MAP P114, D4

Known for its Third Ear music store downstairs (reminiscent

Israeli Opera, Tel Aviv Performing Arts Centre (designed by Ya'akov Rechter)

Azrieli Centre

of the vinyl shop in the film *High Fidelity*), at night Ozen, which means 'ear' in Hebrew, hosts live gigs in its compact venue upstairs. Check the website for event information. (📞03-621-5208; www.ozenbar.com; 48 King George St)

Shopping

Sarona   MARKET

32 🔒 MAP P114, G5

The city's most refined market, swanky Sarona includes two main areas – an outdoor shopping mall and an indoor food market. The outdoor area has offices, restaurants, cafes, fashion stores, galleries and a visitor centre, all housed in restored, 19th-century German Templer houses. The indoor Sarona Market is an arcade featuring global street-food stands and boutique shops to buy fresh meat, fish, cheese and more. (📞centre 03-609-9028, market 03-624-2424; Eliezar Kaplan St, Sarona; 🕑9am-10pm Sun-Thu, 8am-5pm Fri, 9am-11pm Sat; 🛜👫)

Azrieli Centre   MALL

33 🔒 MAP P114, H4

This shopping mall is home to the usual stores such as Zara, Gap and H&M, but the building itself has become something of a Tel Aviv icon. The Azrieli Centre comprises three imposing skyscrapers – square, round and triangle – visible for miles around. There's also a rooftop Azrieli Observatory on the 49th floor (20NIS entry fee). (📞03-608-1199; 132 Menachem Begin

Rd, HaShalom; ☉9.30am-10pm Sun-Thu, to 3pm Fri; 🛜)

Bauhaus Centre GIFTS & SOUVENIRS

34 🅐 MAP P114, C3

This store sells architecture-related books and city plans, including a 1:6000 preservation map and guide to Tel Aviv-Jaffa. It has two Bauhaus walking-tour offerings (each 80NIS per person): one self-guided with a rented audio headset and a two-hour guided walking tour of the same streets at 10am Friday. (☏03-522-0249; www.bauhaus-center.com; 77 Dizengoff St; ☉10am-7pm Sun-Thu, to 2.30pm Fri, to 7.30pm Sat; 🛜)

Mango Tree JEWELLERY

35 🅐 MAP P114, C5

This lively, open-air jewellery atelier specialises in create-your-own pieces – most of which are crafted on the spot – plus ready-to-wear

selections. The owner and staff are friendly as can be, offering helpful opinions on design choices, and the prices are far from extortionate. (☏03-612-2225; www.mangotreeshop.com; 6 Sheinkin St; ☉10am-8pm Sun-Thu, to 4pm Fri)

Dizengoff Centre MALL

36 🅐 MAP P114, D4

Israel's first mall, the Dizengoff Centre is filled with cafes, fast-food joints and major retail chains like Zara, Mango and Adidas. The most walkable place in the City Centre to shop big brands, it also has a cinema, a supermarket, a fitness centre and an indoor pool. A delicious Israeli cooked-food market is held every Friday before Shabbat from 9am to 3pm. There's a large indoor play area on the top floor. (☏03-621-2400; cnr Dizengoff & King George Sts; ☉10am-10pm Sun-Thu, to 5pm Fri, 8-10pm Sat; 👫)

Walking Tour

Rothschild Boulevard Stroll

Bookended by Tel Aviv's first soda kiosk and Habima Sq, Rothschild Boulevard – lined with historical monuments, stylish cafes and Unesco-listed Bauhaus buildings – is the city's most popular stretch for a stroll.

Walk Facts

Start Rothschild Blvd & Herzl St

End Habima Sq

Length 1.5km; two hours

❶ Espresso Bar Kiosk

Kick things off with a caffeine boost at Espresso Bar Kiosk (p143), a local coffee shop franchise that's taken up shop in a restored kiosk where early residents would gather on summer days for *gazoz* (flavoured soda beverages) to beat the heat.

❷ Independence Hall

Continue walking to the statue of Meir Dizengoff, the city's first mayor, on horseback (he was known to commute to City Hall in such a fashion) and Independence Hall (p137) where David Ben-Gurion read the Declaration of Independence to establish Israel as an independent Jewish state on 14 May 1948.

❸ Tel Aviv Founders Monument & Fountain

At the intersection of Nahalat Binyamin St, you'll see the Tel Aviv Founders Monument and Fountain, established in 1949 on the site of the neighbourhood's first water tower.

❹ Haganah Museum

Cross the street to find the Haganah Museum (p137) to the left, which illuminates the history of the paramilitary organisation that preceded today's Israel Defence Forces (IDF).

❺ Refuel at Benedict & Phi

Once you get to Allenby St, there are lots of cafes and restaurants to stop at for a bit of fuel. **Benedict** (☏ 03-686-8657; www.benedict.co.il; 29 Rothschild Blvd; breakfasts from 62NIS; ⊗ 24hr; 🛜 🖊) serves breakfast all day; if it's a cheeky but refreshing cocktail you're after, check out **Phi** (p140) a block and a half away, across from the intersection of Shadal St (where you'll see a single green chair atop a platform) and behind Max Bronner.

❻ Habima Square

Take a rest on any of the benches, bean bags, hammocks or lounge chairs that are available for public use before ending at Habima Square (p116). It's the premier ground of Israeli high culture and a great place to bear witness to the city's famed Bauhaus architecture. The *Hitromemut (Uprise)* Sculpture (p119), better known as the *Three Circles*, by Israeli artist Menashe Kadishman looms in welcome to the Habima Theatre, Charles Bronfman Auditorium and Helena Rubenstein Pavilion.

Explore ✪

South City Centre

Tel Aviv is a vibrant city with many art galleries, cafes, bars and boutiques. But it's here, on the southern fringe, where culture is most pronounced and the city's avant-garde and hipster communities congregate. On weekends, it's where locals flock to enjoy the highly social street scene around the lower part of Rothschild Blvd.

This vast expanse of the city encompasses the Neve Tzedek, Florentin, Nachalat Binyamin and Yemenite Quarter districts. Tucked between the Yemenite Quarter and Nachlat Binyamin is Carmel Market (p130), Tel Aviv's bustling bazaar. From there, head down Allenby St to the city's best boulevard, Rothschild (p126), where shady pedestrian and cycling trails connect historical sights, bars and cafes built into striking Bauhaus buildings. Just east of Rothschild you'll find the serene, cobbled street district of Neve Tzedek; south of here, on the other side of Jaffa Rd, Florentin's scene of counter-culture grit sits in stark contrast with its saturation of street art and edgy galleries.

Getting There & Around

From the city centre, it's a pleasant walk or bike ride down Rothschild Blvd from Habima Sq; Allenby St threads Florentin with the westerly sights south of the city centre. You'll find plenty of taxis and frequent bus service throughout the area.

🚌 Routes 18 and 61 from the city centre run down King George and Allenby Sts before heading west at the Great Synagogue.

South City Centre Map on p134

Vendor at Carmel Market (p130) DNAVEH/SHUTTERSTOCK ©

Top Experience 📷

Try the best boureka in town at the Carmel Market

Tel Aviv's top shuk (market) is a cacophony of sights, smells and sounds. A melting pot of cultures, it's one of the best places in town to try ethnic food favourites. Also a bustling trading post for cheap, fast fashion, it's easy to lose yourself in pursuit of trendy clothes, knock-off watches and sunglasses, kitschy souvenirs and bargain housewares.

◎ MAP P134, F1

HaCarmel St

🕗 8am-late afternoon Sun-Thu, to mid-afternoon Fri

Market Eats

Get past the vendors selling clothes and souvenirs at the market's entrance and make your way towards the end – along the way, you'll find street-food stalls, atmospheric cafes and hole-in-the-wall haunts that serve everything from local classics like shakshuka and hummus to Venezuelan *arepas* and Asian steamed buns.

With its remarkable produce and Mediterranean munchies like halva, olives, baklava and *bourekas* (flaky pastries), it's a utopia for foodies. Butchers and fishmongers sling fresh cuts of meat and seafood, and there's a diverse array of street-food stalls and open-air cafes.

An emerging trend on the Carmel Market scene is local chefs who are moving away from Eurocentric influences and getting back to their Mediterranean and Middle Eastern roots. You'll find eateries serving Turkish, Greek, Yemeni and other ethnic cuisines, all prepared with ingredients sourced straight from the market.

★ Top Tips

○ If it's fresh produce you're after, it's best to visit on Friday afternoon – just before Shabbat – when vendors are more likely to cut deals to move units.

○ Note that Tuesdays and Fridays are the busiest days of the week – if you want to take your time without getting your toes stepped on, pick a different day of the week.

✖ Take a Break

HaBureka (p140), located in the heart of the market, is one of the best places in town to try a *boureka*.

If you're in the mood for kebab, Bar Ochel (p140) is the ideal spot to sit and people watch while you slip into a sweaty meat coma.

Walking Tour 🥾

Florentin Bar Crawl

Florentin, Tel Aviv's creative counter-culture enclave, is a great night out for soaking up some TLV hipster vibes.

Walk Facts

Start Romano, 9 Jaffa Rd
End Satchmo, 2 Vital St
Length 1.2km, five hours

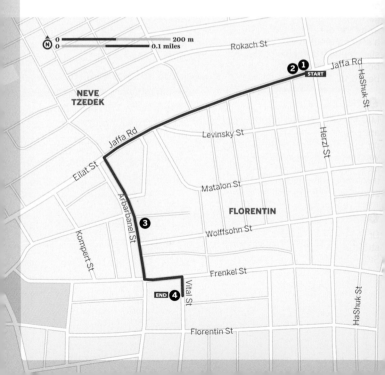

❶ Romano

In true under-the-radar fashion, kick things off with dinner and drinks at Romano (p138), hidden away in the old historic building of the same name. You'll find it behind an unsuspectingly dingy door that faces Jaffa Rd.

❷ Teder.fm

Downstairs is Teder.fm (p143) – which you'll wander down to next for a couple of rounds. Score a table in the open-air courtyard, softly aglow with strings of garden lights. It's easy to while away the hours here, tempted by a second dinner of a rad pizza slice bigger than your head – but boozing in the bowels of Florentin beckons.

❸ Hoodna Bar

Make your way west down Jaffa Rd and hook a left on Arbarbanel St, past the street-art murals that lead you to low-key Hoodna (p143). Kick it here on one of the sofas that's been dragged out into the street or saddle up inside the bar.

❹ Satchmo

Once you're sufficiently sauced, stumble back up the street to Satchmo (p143), one of the oldest

Hoodna Bar

DAN SAVERY RAZ/LONELY PLANET ©

and most beloved old-school neighbourhood bars in Florentin. Don't miss it if you enjoy a stiff scotch or bourbon – with more than 70 varieties to choose from, it's the closest thing to a dedicated whiskey bar you'll find in the area. Ignited by such potent fuel on pour, it's no wonder crowds linger in this place. You'll surely be shoulder to shoulder with the stylish locals, but by this point in the night, things may be so blurry – and the people so beautiful – that you'll hardly mind.

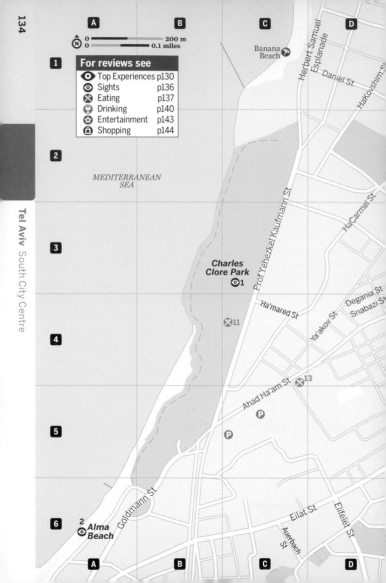

N
0 ——————— 200 m
0 ——————— 0.1 miles

MEDITERRANEAN
SEA

Banana Beach

Herbert Samuel Esplanade

Daniel St

Hakoyshim st

HaCarmel St

Charles Clore Park
◉1

Prof Yehezkel Kaufmann St

Ha'mared St

Degania St

Ya'akov St

Snabazi St

Ahad Ha'am St ✖13

✖11

Goldmann St

Eilat St

Auerbach St

Elifelet St

2
◉ *Alma Beach*

E

YEMENITE QUARTER

Najara St
Rabbi Meir St
Gedera St

F 15 16

Carmel Market

G

H

Melakha St

Sheinken St

1

Hasandlar St

Balfour St

Mazeh St

Nachmani St

2

Kappa St

HaCarmel St

Ha Tavor St

Shefer St

Mohliver St

30

Rambam St

31

22

32

Gruzenberg St

19

Allenby St

Kalisher St

26

Montefiore St

Har Sinai St

8

Ahad Ha'am St

18

23

3

Rothschild Blvd

Ahad Ha'am St

14

Ahad Ha'am St

24

Rothschild Blvd

Nahalat Binyamin St

10

Haganan Museum

5

Independence Hall

Herzl St

Yavne St

Mikveh Israel St

20

4

Yohuda HaLevi St

35

34

33

Pines St

NEVE TZEDEK

Lilienblum St

Yohuda HaLevi St

Rokach St

25

12

Levontin St

HaHashmal St

Jaffa Rd

7

9

5

3

Nachum Gutman Museum of Art

Jaffa Rd

Levinsky St

Matalon St

HaShuk St

21

Zur St

4

Levinsky Spice Market

YL Peretz St

Levinsky St

Chlenov St

27

Wolffsohn St

FLORENTIN

Frenkel St

HaShuk St

Herzl St

HaAliya St

6

Arbarbanel St

Kompert St

Hallat St

28

17

29

Florentin St

Vital St

E

F

G

H

Sights

Charles Clore Park
PARK

1  MAP P134, C3

Sandwiched between Alma Beach and Banana Beach, this 12-hectare stretch of seaside green space is a nice change of pace when you want to marvel at the sunset without sullying yourself with sand. There's a yoga deck, outdoor gym, barbecue areas, playground and a fountain that's great fun to dart around in when the Tel Aviv heat gets too much. (Prof Yehezkel Kaufmann St)

Alma Beach
BEACH

2 MAP P134, A6

With spectacular views across the water to Jaffa, this beach takes the title for Tel Aviv's coolest stretch of sand thanks to the city's hipsters who hang out with their Goldstar beers on Shabbat. It's also home to the hugely popular Manta Ray (p138) restaurant and is the place to pick if you want to round out your sunbathing with some great seafood. (Charles Clore Beach; P)

Nachum Gutman Museum of Art
MUSEUM

3 MAP P134, E5

Take in the multifaceted talents of one of the country's most celebrated creatives through paintings, sculptures and children's book illustrations, all set in a historic home. Some 200 works by 20th-century Israeli artist

Woman Against the Wind sculpture designed by Ilana Goor, Charles Clore Park

Nachum Gutman (1898–1980) are on display in this space that was one of the first 48 structures that formed the nucleus of the charming Neve Tzedek quarter. (☏03-516-1970; www.gutmanmuseum.co.il; 21 Rokach St, Neve Tzedek; adult/child 24/12NIS; ⊙10am-4pm Mon-Thu, to 2pm Fri, to 3pm Sat)

Levinsky Spice Market MARKET

4 ◉ MAP P134, G5

Beloved by celebrity chefs, this aromatic market is a mini-neighbourhood of pantries and stores. Established in the 1920s by Balkan immigrants, this is where local cooks come to source ingredients and is a great place to pick up fresh herbs and spices, dried fruit, stuffed chilli peppers, olive oil, cheese and other goodies – particularly if you feel like avoiding the bustle of Carmel Market. (Shuk Levinsky; www.shuk tlv.co.il; Levinsky St, btwn Herzl St & HaAliya St)

Independence Hall HISTORIC SITE

5 ◉ MAP P134, G4

Though it's still in need of some restoration work, a stop at this site provides some useful historical insight. Originally the home of Meir Dizengoff, one of the city's founding fathers and its first mayor, it was here, on 14 May 1948, that David Ben-Gurion declared the establishment of the State of Israel. Entry includes a short introductory film and a tour of the room where Israel's Declaration

of Independence was signed. (Beit Haatzmaut; ☏03-510-6426; http://eng.ihi.org.il; 16 Rothschild Blvd; adult/student/child 24/18/16NIS; ⊙9am-5pm Sun-Thu, to 2pm Fri)

Haganah Museum MUSEUM

6 ◉ MAP P134, G3

Splendidly located on Rothschild Blvd, this museum chronicles the formation and activities of the Haganah, the paramilitary organisation that was the forerunner of today's Israel Defence Forces (IDF). A civilian guerrilla force protecting kibbutzim (Jewish farms and cooperatives) from attack in the 1920s and '30s, the Haganah went on to assist in the illegal entry of more than 100,000 Jews into Palestine after the British government's 1939 white paper restricting immigration. After WWII Haganah fighters carried out anti-British operations. (☏03-560-8624; 23 Rothschild Blvd; adult/student & child 15/10NIS; ⊙8am-4pm Sun-Thu)

Eating

Taizu FUSION $$$

7 ✗ MAP P134, H5

Indian, Chinese, Thai, Vietnamese and Cambodian flavours shine through the elements at this upscale 'AsiaTerranean' fusion restaurant, and a dinner here is one of Tel Aviv's finest. Start with selections from the 'water' or 'wood' sections of the menu – the Shanghai veal cheek soup dumplings are especially good – and finish with octopus korma from 'earth' or fried sea bass from 'metal'. (03-522-5005; www.taizu. co.il; 23 Menachem Begin Rd; mains 88-168NIS; 6.30-11.30pm Mon-Thu, from 6pm Fri, from 7pm Sat & Sun; lunch noon-3.30pm Thu & Fri, from 12.30pm Sat)

Port Sa'id   MIDDLE EASTERN $$

8 MAP P134, G3

The mothership for inner-city hipsters, this restaurant-bar next to the Great Synagogue is decorated with a library of vinyl records on wooden shelves and has a coterie of heavily tattooed regulars. There's good Middle Eastern–accented food on offer and lots of drink choices. (5 Har Sinai St; mains from 44NIS; noon-late;)

Dalida   FUSION $$$

9 MAP P134, G5

One of Florentin's finest, Dalida is named after and inspired by the former Miss Egypt and iconic '60s singer who, like the food here, blended Arab, Italian and French styles. High-class but homey, Dalida offers a half-price menu from 5pm to 7pm Sunday to Thursday. Try the Arabic cabbage with seared calamari or lamb, pistachios and halloumi kebab. (03-536-9627; http://en.dalidatlv. co.il; 7 Zvulun St; mains 84-142NIS; 5pm-2am Sun-Thu, from noon Fri & Sat;)

Tamara   ICE CREAM $

10 MAP P134, G3

Like its other branch on Ben Yehuda St (p120), Tamara offers the best frozen yoghurt in Tel Aviv. Located on the corner of Rothschild Blvd and Nahalat Binyamin St, it's in the heart of the city's nightlife district and makes a great late-night dessert. If you're feeling naughty, try the hot chocolate sauce; healthier choices include tapioca or granola with fruit. (03-517-5777; www.facebook.com/tamara.telaviv; 19 Rothschild Blvd; small/medium/large cup 26/32/38NIS; 10am-midnight)

Manta Ray   SEAFOOD $$$

11 MAP P134, C4

It's stylish, casual and at the beach – the perfect Tel Avivian triumvirate. On the slope directly above Alma Beach (p136), this is the summer breakfast and lunch venue of choice for locals and tourists alike, so be sure to book (specify an outside table with a view). Try an omelette at breakfast and fish at other times of the day. (03-517-4773; www.mantaray. co.il; southern Tel Aviv Promenade; breakfast 39-69NIS, mains 75-185NIS; 9am-11pm;)

Romano   FUSION $$

12 MAP P134, F5

A hidden hipster gem, the entrance to Romano is deceiving. Behind the graffiti and gates, through a courtyard and up a

Levinsky Spice Market (p137)

staircase, this restaurant is one of the hottest spots in south TLV, one of chef Eyal Shani's quirky creations. Bruce Lee film posters adorn the walls as the young and hungry tuck into experimental and classic dishes. (☏054-317-7051; www.facebook.com/romanotlv; 9 Jaffa Rd, Florentin; mains 49-98NIS; ⏰6pm-3am; ☏)

Dallal
FRENCH $$$

13 ⊗ MAP P134, C4

For one of Tel Aviv's best brunches, head here on Saturday between noon and 6pm, when the garden tables are full of locals noshing on organic egg dishes, such as the roasted eggplant shakshuka with spinach, tomato coulis and goat yoghurt. Dinner in the slightly twee dining room is a more formal affair, featuring conservative, French-influenced meat and fish dishes. (☏03-510-9292; www.dallal.info; 10 Shabazi St, Neve Tzedek; breakfast 44-65NIS, mains 82-167NIS; ⏰noon-11.30pm Sun-Thu, from 9am Fri & Sat; ☏)

Meshek Barzilay
CAFE $$

14 ⊗ MAP P134, F3

Vegetarians and vegans are well catered for in Tel Aviv, but this place goes that extra mile when it comes to making them happy. One of only two restaurants we found serving organic free-range eggs (bravo!), it has plenty of interesting Indian- and Asian-influenced dishes on its menu and some great breakfast choices.

Regulars swear by the vegan farm breakfast. (☏03-516-6329; www. meshekbarzilay.co.il; 6 Ahad Ha'am St, Neve Tzedek; mains 52-68NIS; ☺8am-11pm Sun-Fri, from 9am Sat; 🛜🍴)

HaBureka
MIDDLE EASTERN $

15 🍴 MAP P134, F1

The sounds of Carmel Market are many – but the most audible, in the heart of the market, is that of a sole man shouting 'bourekas, bourekas!' from a simple stall. The wail alone is enough to induce pause, but with a single bite of one of these airy, flaky filled pastries, you'll be glad you did. (☏054-533-2337; www.facebook. com/burika.carmelmarket; 42 HaCarmel St, Carmel Market; bourekas from 10NIS; ☺10am-6pm Sun-Fri)

Bar Ochel
MEDITERRANEAN $$

16 🍴 MAP P134, F1

A lively bastion of meaty Mediterranean delights, Ochel (simply meaning 'food' in Hebrew) epitomises the concept of locally sourced cuisine. The ingredients travel mere metres to get to your plate – chefs procure all produce right in Carmel Market, so the fantastic kebabs (they stake claim to the best in Tel Aviv) and hearty salads are as fresh as it gets. (☏050-915-7756; www. facebook.com/pg/carmelmeatbar; 38 HaCarmel St, Carmel Market; mains 25-62NIS; ☺9am-7.30pm Sun-Tue, to 11pm Wed-Thu, 8am-5.30pm Fri)

Beit Lechem Hummus
MIDDLE EASTERN $

17 🍴 MAP P134, E6

The free self-service tshai nana (mint tea) is a nice touch, but Florentin regulars are drawn here solely on the strength of the hummus. Choose from fuul (with mashed and spiced fava beans) or masabacha (with chickpeas and warm tahina) versions, and consider ordering an egg topping (2NIS). (5 Florentin St; hummus 18NIS; ☺10am-9pm Sun-Thu, to 4pm Fri; 🍴)

Drinking

Phi
BAR

18 🍺 MAP P134, H3

Mainstream and counterculture youngsters flock to this sleek, open-air garden bar for their famous colour-categorised fresh juices that can be spiked with your pick of poison. We dig the 'Green' – apple, lime and ginger plus gin, adorned with a sprig of mint harvested from the fresh herb garden. They sure do go down easy... good thing they're 'healthy.' (☏050-937-9393; www. alphabet-club.com/phi; 54 Ahad Ha'am St; ☺6pm-6am Sun-Thu, 24hr Fri & Sat)

Bicicletta
BEER GARDEN

19 🍺 MAP P134, F2

A vibrant, young bar on Nahalat Binyamin St, Bicicletta (Italian for 'bicycle') has one of the best patio gardens in town. The food is great – eclectic dishes include the smoked turkey sandwich with brie, pork belly with cauliflower and date honey, and its signature homemade aubergine fries. Happy hour is from 5.30pm to 8pm. Look for the bicycle in the window. (☎03-643-3097; www.facebook.com/BiciclettaTLV; 29 Nahalat Binyamin St; ☺6pm-2am Sun-Thu, from noon Fri & Sat; 🛜)

Kuli Alma   BAR

20 🚇 MAP P134, H4

Mystical and just downright cool, Kuli Alma is a TLV nightlife institution with an emphasis on art and music. Behind the unimposing entrance, locals and not-so-locals mingle on the patio dotted with plants, graffiti and an outdoor gal-

lery. There's a vegetarian menu, and it hosts an eclectic mix of DJ and live music nights. (☎03-656-5155; http://kulialma.com; 10 Mikveh Israel St; ☺10pm-5am; 🛜)

Café Levinsky   CAFE

21 🚇 MAP P134, G5

Find refreshing relief from the sweltering Tel Aviv heat here with *gazoz*, an old-fashioned drink of simple syrup and soda water. Illuminated jars of fermented fruits and botanicals line the shelves of this Levinsky Market favourite – housed in a tiny former storage unit – where the bespoke beverages are concocted based on the barista's whims and what's seasonally appropriate. (☎058-448-8480; www.facebook.com/levinsky41; 41 Levinsky

Alma Beach (p136)

Musicians playing at Nahalat Binyamin Crafts Market (p144)

St, Florentin; ⏰6.30am-7pm Sun-Thu, to 5pm Fri)

Prince

ROOFTOP BAR

22 🚇 MAP P134, F2

For years, this place was one of Tel Aviv's best-kept secrets: an amazing rooftop bar on the corner of the Nahalat Binyamin Crafts Market. But now the secret is well and truly out and the Prince (*Ha-Nasich* in Hebrew) is packed to the brim with people. Like all good Tel Aviv bars, it has a dark and dingy entrance (with some pretty weird graffiti). (📞058-606-1818; www. facebook.com/theprincetlv; 18 Nahalat Binyamin St; ⏰5pm-1am Sat-Thu, noon-7pm Fri)

Alphabet

CLUB

23 🚇 MAP P134, H3

Underground techno and house tunes spin at this intimate club that welcomes a diverse crowd of party goers. There are two rooms – Alpha, which is near the entrance, keeps beats a little more tame than the Gamma room, which you'll find past the corridor of tall, metal-doored toilets. When your senses get assaulted by frenetic strobe lights, palpitation-inducing bass and an explosion of confetti, you know that you've arrived. (www.alphabet-club.com; 54 Ahad Ha'am St; ⏰11pm-8am Wed & Thu, 24hr Fri & Sat)

Espresso Bar Kiosk
COFFEE

24 MAP P134, F3

This branch of the local franchise serves up a little jolt of history with your Java – it's housed in a restored structure that was once the city's first *gazoz* (soda) kiosk and the hub of the early Tel Aviv ian summer social scene. There's no *gazoz* on tap today, but you'll get great coffees and fresh pastries in a nostalgic atmosphere. (📞03-510-8915; www.espressobar. com; 82 Rothschild Blvd; ⏰7am-midnight Sat-Thu, to 6pm Fri)

Teder.fm
BAR

25 MAP P134, F4

Born as an internet radio station and roaming bar, Teder.fm has set down roots in the disused Romano building. Still broadcasting its unique underground radio to the world on its website, the bar itself is on the ground floor of the same courtyard as the restaurant Romano (p138). (http://teder.fm/en; 9 Jaffa Rd, Florentin; ⏰7pm-late Mon-Fri, from 4pm Sat; 📶)

Shpagat
GAY & LESBIAN

26 MAP P134, G2

A hip gay bar, Shpagat attracts big crowds most nights thanks to a vibrant, all-are-welcome vibe and stadium step-style seating that acts as the perfect perch for those with wandering eyes. In the early evening, it's a peaceful, intimate spot to grab a drink, but later on the DJs take over

and the volume goes up a notch or 10. (📞03-560-1785; 43 Nahalat Binyamin St; ⏰7pm-late Sat-Thu, noon-5pm Fri)

Hoodna Bar
BAR

27 MAP P134, E6

Hoodna ('truce' in Arabic) is a carpenter's workshop zone by day but transforms itself at night, when tables and sofas are dragged into the street to create a chilled-out drinking space. Inside there are almost-daily live or DJ sets. (📞03-518-4558; 13 Arbarbanel St, Florentin; ⏰7pm-4am Sat-Thu, from 9pm Fri; 📶)

Satchmo
BAR

28 MAP P134, E6

The longest-running and possibly best loved bar in Florentin, Satchmo has an old-school neighbourhood vibe and a fantastic selection of more than 70 whiskeys. A DJ spins classic and alternative rock every night. We particularly like its mantra: 'bad decisions make great stories'. (2 Vital St, Florentin; ⏰6pm-late)

Entertainment

Barby
LIVE MUSIC

29 MAP P134, F6

This Tel Aviv institution at the southernmost point of the city is a favourite venue for reggae, electronica, funk and alternative bands. Occasionally hosts big-name acts, and the vibe is always positive with a capital 'P'. (☎03-518-8123; www.barby.co.il; 52 Kibbutz Galuyot St)

Beit HaAmudim
JAZZ

30 ⭐ MAP P134, F1

Tel Aviv's intimate live jazz venue welcomes a disparate crowd to its almost nightly gigs, which kick off at 9.30pm. Entry fee for gigs is 5NIS per musician, so if you see a band of five people, you pay 25NIS. Close to Carmel Market, it functions as a cafe during the day. (☎03-510-9228; www.facebook.com/BeitHaamudim; 14 Rambam St; ⏰noon-2am Sun, Mon, Wed & Thu, 9am-3am Tue & Fri, 7pm-3am Sat)

Shopping

Nahalat Binyamin Crafts Market
MARKET

31 🔒 MAP P134, F1

Open on Tuesdays and Fridays, this is the city's premier arts and crafts market. Visitors can expect a plethora of stalls selling paintings, ornaments and other handmade crafts, plus the odd street performer. It's also a great place to grab a bite to eat followed by an ice cream from Arte. (www.nachlatbinyamin.com; Nahalat Binyamin St; ⏰10am-5pm Tue, 10am to 4.30pm Fri)

Contour
JEWELLERY

32 🔒 MAP P134, F2

Contour was founded by two award-winning Israeli designers,

Lior Shulak-Hai and Galit Barak, in 2015. Located near Nahalat Binyamin Crafts Market, Contour creates bespoke, handmade jewellery that's unique in its bold and beautiful shapes. (☎03-654-2270; www.contour-studio.com; 25 Gruzenberg St; ⏰10am-6pm Sun-Thu, to 2pm Fri)

Sipur Pashut
BOOKS

33 🔒 MAP P134, E4

Bookshops don't get much cuter than this. Sipur Pashut (meaning 'simple story') is a tiny shop filled from floor to ceiling with quality Hebrew and English literature. Set right in the heart of Neve Tzedek, it is also a venue for poetry readings, book launches and children's stories. It publishes the Israeli version of the world-renowned *Granta* literary magazine. (☎03-510-7040; www.sipurpashut.com/english; 36 Shabazi St, Neve Tzedek; ⏰10am-8pm Sun-Thu, 9.30am-4pm Fri)

Chomer Tov
CERAMICS

34 🔒 MAP P134, E4

A cooperative of 15 ceramic artists, Chomer Tov (meaning 'good material') is both a small gallery and a shop. A dynamic space, it features both functional (eg bowls and cups) and imaginative designs alike, as well as modern Judaica. If you're searching for a unique, handmade souvenir with local flair, this is a fantastic place

Itamar Levy on stage at Barby (p143)

to get it. (📞03-516-6220; www.chomertov.co.il; 27 Shabazi St, Neve Tzedek; ⏰10am-8pm Sun-Thu, to 5pm Fri)

Agas & Tamar
JEWELLERY

35 📍 MAP P134, E4

Pass through an old metal door to discover the workshop and retail space of Einat Agassi and Tamar Harel-Klein, who use gold and silver to create 'storytelling jewellery' inspired by a theme or historical artefact (coin, nail, seal etc). (📞03-516-8421; www.agasandtamar.com; 43 Shabazi St, Neve Tzedek; ⏰10am-7pm Sun-Thu, to 3pm Fri)

Explore ◎
North Tel Aviv

Here in the north, things operate at a more relaxed pace – and in a city as laid back as Tel Aviv, that's saying a lot. With its shaded streets lined with casual cafes, it's where young professionals and families dwell, spending weekends on the beach, in the expansive green parks and at the lively old port.

Dive into Tel Aviv's north with a visit to the Old Port (p152). Pick up picnic provisions at the Old Port Farmers Market (p155) and then head to Hilton (p152) or Metzitzim Beach (p152) for a blast of Mediterranean sunshine, or to Park HaYarkon (p148) to lounge in the grass with the locals. North of the Yarkon River is the suburb of Ramat Aviv and Tel Aviv University, where you'll find this area's museums – check out Beit Hatfutsot (p151; the Museum of the Jewish People) and the Eretz Israel Museum (p152) for fascinating insight into Jewish culture and history.

Getting There & Around

It's relatively easy to reach north Tel Aviv's sights on foot or bicycle from the city centre. Taxis can get you here with no problem and many buses have routes that run through the area on the way to the northern suburbs.

🚌 From the Central Station, take routes 4, 104 and 204 to get to the beaches and Port; routes 189 and 289 run along Ibn Gabriol St – get off at Milano Square for Park HaYarkon.

North Tel Aviv Map on p150

Hilton Beach (p152) FOTOKON/SHUTTERSTOCK ©

Top Experience 📷
Get active in Park HaYarkon

For a break from the hustle and bustle of the city, head north to the impressive Park HaYarkon, Tel Aviv's green lung breathing serenity into the city. It's set along the banks of the Yarkon River – the longest coastal waterway in Israel, which winds 28km from its source just north of Petah Tikva to the Mediterranean Sea.

◎ MAP P150, D2

Ganei Yehoshua

www.park.co.il

Rokach Blvd

Activities

Joggers, cyclists, dog walkers and parents pushing prams pack the park's trails daily, and its sprawling swaths of verdant grass are an inviting scene for relaxing with a picnic when you're ready for a break.

If its adrenaline you're after, you'll find that too. The park's multisport complex, **Sportek** (03-699-0307; www.park.co.il; rock climbing from 55NIS; 9am-10.30pm Sun-Thu, 2-8pm Fri, 10am-9pm Sat), has everything from a rock-climbing wall and trampolines to ball courts and skateboard ramps (balls and rollerblades are available for hire). There are indeed lots of ways to get high on life in this park – including a hot-air-balloon attraction called the **TLV Balloon** (03-558-9722; www.tlv-balloon.co.il; adult/child 80/55NIS; 9am-9pm Sat-Thu, to 5pm Fri).

You can play a round of minigolf or hire a variety of watercraft, including paddle boats, motor boats, kayaks and row boats, and take to the open waters of the lake at the eastern end of the park. If you'd rather stick to shore, remote-control model boats are also available to take for a spin.

Kids will get a kick out of the park's petting zoo, complete with a reptile corner, and **Meymadion Water Park** (03-642-2777; www.meymadion.co.il; adult/child under 2 119NIS/free; 9am-4.30pm daily Jun-Aug, 9am-4.30pm Sat only to mid-Sep), which has fun slides and a wave pool.

★ **Top Tips**

o The Usishkin Beili Bridge, connecting the north and south banks of the Yarkon River, is a great place to take in the sunset.

o While expansive lawns are great to chill out on, you can really unplug by meandering through the park's themed gardens, including a 4-hectare cactus garden featuring some 3500 species – one of the largest of its kind in the world.

o The park regularly hosts events, including performances by the Israel Philharmonic Orchestra and the **Israeli Opera** (www.israel-opera.co.il; Jul/Aug); check the website (www.park.co.il) for details.

✕ **Take a Break**

It's best to pack a picnic as there's not much in the way of refreshments inside. Pick up some goodies from the Old Port Farmers Market (p155), close to the park's western edge.

Tel Aviv North Tel Aviv

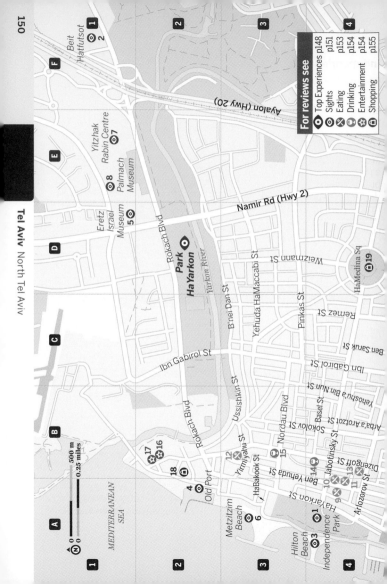

MEDITERRANEAN SEA

0   500 m
0   0.25 miles

Beit Hatfutsot

Yitzhak Rabin Centre

Palmach Museum

Eretz Israel Museum

Ayalon (Hwy 20)

Namir Rd (Hwy 2)

Park HaYarkon

Yarkon River

Rokach Blvd

Ibn Gabirol St

Ussishkin St

B'nei Dan St

Yehuda HaMaccabi St

Weizmann St

Pinkas St

Remez St

HaMedina Sq

Ben Saruk St

Ibn Gabirol St

Yehoshu'a Bin Nun St

Arba'a Artozot St

Basel St

Sokolov St

Nordau Blvd

Jabotinsky St

Dizengoff St

Arlozorov St

Old Port

Metzitzim Beach

HaBakook St

Yirmiyahu St

Ben Yehuda St

HaYarkon St

Independence Park

Hilton Beach

Sights

Independence Park

PARK

1 ⊙ MAP P150, A4

Nothing to do with Independence Hall on the other side of town, this beautiful seafront park is great for its Mediterranean views and plenty of grass to run around, throw a frisbee or have a picnic. Like most of Tel Aviv's public spaces, it's popular with dog walkers and is the venue for children's birthday parties on weekends. Next to the Hilton Hotel, it also has a well-equipped children's play area with swings, slides and climbing frames. (Gan Ha'atzma'ut)

Beit Hatfutsot

MUSEUM

2 ⊙ MAP P150, F1

Once known as the Diaspora Museum but revamped as the Museum of the Jewish People, Beit Hatfutsot is located on the leafy campus of Tel Aviv University. Opened in 1978, the museum recounts the epic story of the Jewish exile and global Jewish diaspora using objects, photographs, audiovisual presentations and databases. Permanent exhibitions include Heroes, an interactive exhibit on Jewish greats such as Einstein (for children), and Hallelujah!, displaying intricate models of synagogues from past and present. (Museum of the Jewish People; ☏03-745-7808; www.bh.org.il; Gate 2, Tel Aviv University, 2 Klausner

Old Port area (p152)

St, Ramat Aviv; adult/child under 5yr 45NIS/free; ⏰10am-7pm Sun-Wed, to 10.30pm Thu, 9am-2pm Fri, to 3pm Sat; 🅿; 🚌Dan 7, 13, 25, 45)

Hilton Beach
BEACH

3 ◎ MAP P150, A4

Named after the nearby hotel, Hilton Beach is divided into three parts: the city's unofficial gay beach is in the middle, the dog-walkers' beach is to the north (it's the only beach where dogs are officially allowed), and surfers hang ten near the breakwater in the south. This bay is also used for kayaking and windsurfing activities and lessons.

Old Port
PORT

4 ◎ MAP P150, A2

The Old Port is popular with families wandering around its waterfront shops, restaurants and cafes. A covered organic farmers market (p155) also attracts locals looking for their fresh vegetables, pasta and seafood. After dark and on weekends, hordes of clubbers descend on the area's strip of bars and nightclubs after midnight. (Namal; www.namal. co.il; 🅿)

Eretz Israel Museum
MUSEUM

5 ◎ MAP P150, D1

Incorporating the archaeological excavations of Tel Qasile, an ancient port city dating from the 12th century BCE, this museum sports a huge and varied range of exhibits and deserves at least half a day for those who appreciate curious relics of bygone eras. Sights include pavilions filled with glass and coins, a reconstructed flour mill and olive-oil plant, an ethnography and folklore collection, and a garden built around a gorgeous Byzantine bird mosaic. A planetarium is among the other attractions. (Land of Israel Museum; ☏03-641-5244; www.eretzmuseum. org.il; 2 Chaim Levanon St, Ramat Aviv; adult/student/child under 18yr 52/35NIS/free, incl planetarium adult/child 84/32NIS; ⏰10am-4pm Sat, Mon & Wed, to 8pm Tue & Thu, to 2pm Fri, planetarium shows Mon-Thu & Sat; 🅿; 🚌Dan 7, 13, 24, 25, 45, 127)

Metzitzim Beach
BEACH

6 ◎ MAP P150, A3

Named after a 1972 comedy film, Hof Metzitzim (which – uncharacteristic of the beach itself – translates as the sleazy 'Peeping Tom Beach') is actually a family-friendly bay with a small play area for children. It also hosts Friday afternoon beach parties during summer.

Yitzhak Rabin Centre
MUSEUM

7 ◎ MAP P150, E1

Established in 1997 to promote democratic values, narrow socioeconomic gaps and address social divisiveness, this centre is also home to the Israeli Museum, which includes 150 films and 1500 photographs telling the story of modern Israel's struggle for peace with its neighbours. Visitors can take a self-guided tour using a multilanguage audio device or book in advance to join a guided tour in Hebrew or English. (☏03-745-3358; www.rabincenter.org.il; 14 Chaim Levanon St; self-guided tour adult/student & child 50/25NIS; guided tour 60/35NIS; ⏱9am-5pm Sun, Mon & Wed, to 7pm Tue & Thu, to 2pm Fri; 🅿; 🚌Dan 7, 29, 85)

Palmach Museum   MUSEUM

8 ◉ MAP P150, E1

The story of the Palmach, from its establishment in 1941 until the end of the Arab–Israeli War of 1948, is the focus of this multimedia museum. Starting in a memorial hall for Palmach members who died fighting for the establishment of the State of Israel, a Hebrew speaking guide takes visitors on a tour that focuses on the stories of individual members who fought with this elite Haganah strike force. Headphones provide translations into other languages. (☏03-643-6393; www.palmach.org.il; 10 Haim Levanon St, Ramat Aviv; adult/child 30/20NIS; ⏱by appointment only Sun Fri; 🅿)

Eating

Barbunia   SEAFOOD $$

9 ✖ MAP P150, A4

Going strong for nearly three decades, Barbunia is older than most of Tel Aviv's residents. The no-frills, paper tablecloths add to the charm of this fish restaurant. All mains come with a seemingly endless stream of salads, fried vegetables, bread basket and hummus. Sea bream or mixed fried shrimps and calamari are highly recommended, washed down with a local beer. (☏03-527-6965; 163 Ben Yehuda St; mains 58-86NIS; ⏱noon-11pm)

Dosa Bar   INDIAN $$

10 ✖ MAP P150, A4

Indian, kosher, vegan and gluten-free – Dosa Bar is all of the above. This small restaurant with friendly staff specialises in dosa (Indian pancakes) served sweet or savoury – the masala dosa is particularly good. It also does Indian breakfasts on Friday if you fancy starting the weekend with some spice. (☏03-659-1961; www.facebook.com/Dosabar; 188 Ben Yehuda St; mains from 42NIS; ⏱noon-11pm Sun-Thu, 11am-4pm Fri; ✖)

Shila   SEAFOOD $$$

11 ✖ MAP P150, A4

Only a castanet click or two away from the beach, Sharo Cohen's Spanish-inspired seafood restaurant offers an array of vividly coloured and robustly flavoured small plates and grilled main courses. Those in the know tend to start with a few carpaccio and tartar shareables and then graze on the vegetable, fish and seafood dishes on offer. (☏03-522-1224; www.shila-rest.co.il; 182 Ben Yehuda St; mains 86-168NIS; ⏱12.30pm-midnight Fri-Wed, to 1am Thu)

Tel Aviv North Tel Aviv

Nam
THAI $$

12 ⊗ MAP P150, B3

It may sound like a Vietnamese restaurant, but Nam is very much a Thai cook house with tasty classic dishes and hearty portions. Advance booking is strongly advised, as it's hugely popular with Tel Avivians looking for their next green curry or pad thai. Nam offers 10% off all mains during its business lunch hours. (☑03-670-8050; www.namrestaurant.co.il; 275 Dizengoff St; mains 65-77NIS; ⊗12.30-5pm & 6pm-midnight; 🛜)

Urban Shaman
HEALTH FOOD $$

13 ⊗ MAP P150, B4

While juice bars are easy to come by in Tel Aviv, the folks behind Urban Shaman – a naturopath and journalist duo – get a green star for their carefully curated selection of cold-pressed organic juice blends and wellness shots served up in sustainable glass bottles. Pair your tonic with a superfood bowl, salad or light breakfast. (☑03-752-1102; www.urbanshaman.co.il; 210 Dizengoff St; juices from 26NIS, mains 34-55NIS; ⊗8am-9pm Sun-Thu, 8.30am-4pm Fri)

Drinking

223
COCKTAIL BAR

14 🍸 MAP P150, B4

Pioneering Tel Aviv's spirits scene, award-winning Israeli mixologist Ariel Leizgold opened 223 in 2008, long before the city caught on to the trend of upmarket watering holes. The first and longest-running cocktail bar in town, it's the premiere choice for top-notch classic cocktails in an inviting, sophisticated atmosphere. (☑03-544-6537; www.223.co.il; 223 Dizengoff St; ⊗6pm-4am Sat-Thu, from 7pm Fri)

Double Standard
COCKTAIL BAR

15 🍸 MAP P150, B3

The folks behind pharmacy-inspired Spicehaus bring swanky spirits to Tel Aviv's north with a space that's a cocktail supply shop by day and a chic-but-chill bar at night. No matter the hour, presentation rules – pick up an IV bag of Bloody Mary mix in the shop or sip a cocktail from the mouth of a shark at the bar. (☑03-555-0966; www.facebook.com/dsbarshop; 247 Dizengoff St; ⊗6pm-3am)

Entertainment

Shablul Jazz Club
JAZZ

16 🎭 MAP P150, B2

Live jazz, blues, salsa and world music takes centre stage at this intimate venue on the Old Port almost nightly. Check the website and Facebook page (www.facebook.com/shabluljazz) for an events calendar. (☑03-546-1891; www.shabluljazz.com; Hangar 13, Old Port)

Me on the Mic
KARAOKE

17 🎭 MAP P150, B2

Pick from a choice of different-sized private rooms at this fun

Palmach Museum (p153), designed by Zvi Hecker and Rafi Segal

karaoke bar. It has a full list of songs in English, Spanish and Hebrew. Costs range from basic room hire and two drinks (100NIS) to the Back Stage pass (220NIS), which includes full dinner and unlimited drinks. (www.meonthemic.co.il; 4 Yosef Yekutieli, Hangar 27, Old Port; per person 100-220NIS; ⊙4pm-1.30am)

Shopping

Old Port
Farmers Market   MARKET

18 🔒 MAP P150, B2

Delicious farmers market set in a restored hangar on the Old Port of Tel Aviv; it sometimes spills out into stands at the entrance.

Like all popular markets in Israel, it's based on food and drink, with plenty of options for hungry wanderers. (☎077 541 1303; http://shukhanamal.co.il/english; Hangar 12, Old Port; ⊙9am-4pm Sun, to 8pm Mon-Thu & Sat, 7am-5pm Fri)

Kikar
HaMedina   FASHION & ACCESSORIES

19 🔒 MAP P150, D4

The circular Kikar HaMedina (which means State Sq) is actually just a large roundabout with grass in the centre, popular with dog walkers. Its perimeter is the place to fulfil all your Gucci, Tag Heuer and Versace needs. (HaMedina Sq)

Top Experience 📷
Watch some *matkot* on the beach

When the sun is out – and especially during the summer months – the 14km-long string of sandy beaches between Tel Aviv Port and Jaffa has an all-pervading pull. City residents head here to laze on the sand, play matkot *(paddle ball), frolic in the surf, and stroll, run or cycle along the beachside promenade.*

Many buses stop near the beaches – check the tourist office for timetables.

Bograshov St, Frishman St and Gordon St lead directly to their respective namesake beaches.

Gordon Beach

Equipped with sun loungers, ice-cream shops, an outdoor gym and beach restaurants, this beach is popular with Tel Avivians and tourists. On Saturdays, you'll likely see group folk dancing on the boardwalk. The **Gordon Swimming Pool** (03-762-3300; www.gordon-pool.co.il; Tel Aviv Marina; adult/student & child Sun-Fri 69/59NIS, Sat 79/70NIS; 6am-9pm Mon-Thu, to 7pm Fri, 7am-6pm Sat, 1.30-9pm Sun;) is at the nearby marina.

Frishman Beach

Frishman Beach is the widest stretch of sand in Tel Aviv. There's plenty of space on the sand and good access to the swimming area. It's in front of the rainbow-coloured Dan Hotel building and has large wooden gazebos for shade.

Bograshov Beach

One of Tel Aviv's most popular beaches, Bograshov is part of a party central strip along with Gordon and Frishman. Relatively quiet during the week, on weekends it overflows with bronze-bodied locals and slightly sunburnt tourists.

Hilton Beach

Named after the nearby hotel, Hilton Beach (p152) is divided into three parts: the city's unofficial gay beach in the middle, the dog walkers' beach to the north (it's the only beach where dogs are officially allowed) and surfers hang near the breakwater in the south. This bay is also used for kayaking and windsurfing.

★ Top Tips

o Take note of the flags in the sand that indicate water conditions: white and blue mean calm currents; red signals choppy waves and strong currents, so use caution; black means it's too dangerous to enter the water at all.

o Beach-furniture hire is regulated by the municipality: chairs cost 6NIS, an umbrella 6NIS and a lounger 12NIS.

o For a break from the sand, head to the Gordon Swimming Pool or Charles Clore Park (p136), where you can enjoy the green space but still soak up the beach vibes.

✗ Take a Break

Manta Ray (p138) on Alma Beach is great for seafood with a sunset view.

Explore ◉

Jaffa (Yafo)

Jaffa, a separate enclave from Tel Aviv with its own ancient, 4000-plus-year-long history, is home to more Arab than Jewish residents and has a completely different atmosphere. Amble along arched alleyways, past stone structures aglow with golden light to find a hive of charming art galleries and creative makers' spaces, along with bohemian bars and buzzing restaurants.

Browse the flea market (p160), where you'll find locals selling their once-loved wares. If used knick-knacks and threads aren't your thing, the surrounding storefronts include fashion, jewellery and home décor boutiques. Next, roam the hilltop Old City – begin at the visitors centre (p163) and see partially excavated remains from the Hellenistic and Roman era and learn about Jaffa's history in a virtual experience. Finally, amble over to Jaffa Port for a seafood feast at Old Man & the Sea (p164).

Getting There & Around

If you're up for a seaside stroll, Jaffa is about a 25-minute walk from Tel Aviv's central beaches, down the promenade and through Charles Clore Park. Jaffa is concentrated and easily walkable; all the sights are spread over a small area that spans from the flea market on the district's eastern edge to the port just 15 minutes to the southwest.

🚌 Number 10 and 18 from the city centre and number 41 from the central bus terminal stop on Sderot Yerushalayim, the southern extension of the seafront Herbert Samuel Esplanade.

Jaffa (Yafo) Map on p162

Top Experience 📷
Find an antique treasure at Jaffa Flea Market

In a place as ancient as Jaffa, antiques are a given. The old city's famous flea market is one of the best places in the area to score such previously loved bargains, but the treasures don't end there. All around the traditional market are lifestyle boutiques that feature unique gifts, bespoke jewellery and fashionable threads from modern, local designers.

◎ MAP P162, C3

Shuk HaPishpeshim

🕐 stalls 10am-3pm Sun-Wed & Fri, to late Thu

🚌 Dan 10, 18, 25, 41

Score by Bargaining

As with many markets across the world, prices here are often set rather high – but haggling isn't considered rude (despite any disposition of offence you may encounter). If the initial price of an item is more than you'd like to pay, don't be afraid to throw out a lower figure.

If, after a bit of bargaining, you're still not getting down to a price you'd prefer to pay, try walking away slowly – if the vendor beckons you back, they're likely willing to keep the negotiation going in your favour. Put on your best poker face – and it helps to show a small degree of apathy if you really are just curious about an item but don't want to be pressured into a sale.

Modern Makers

Though residents and tourists alike shop the flea market for antiques, you can pick up something a bit more modern to remember your trip at Saga (p166), a design shop selling wares made by local creators.

★ Top Tips

o Don't be put off by piles of clothes and wares displayed on the ground – digging through the personal belongings of the locals is half the fun.

o Pack hand wipes or sanitiser – rummaging through piles for gems comes with its fair share of dust and grime.

o Catch busking and other demonstrations – like giant bubble blowing – around the market, especially on Thursdays and Fridays.

✕ Take a Break

When you've had your fill of retail therapy in the flea market, chill out with a beer and a bite at Shaffa (p165). If you've worked up an appetite but aren't ready to give up the pursuit of prowling for treasure, eat at Puaa (p165), where everything in the cafe is for sale.

Tel Aviv Jaffa (Yafo)

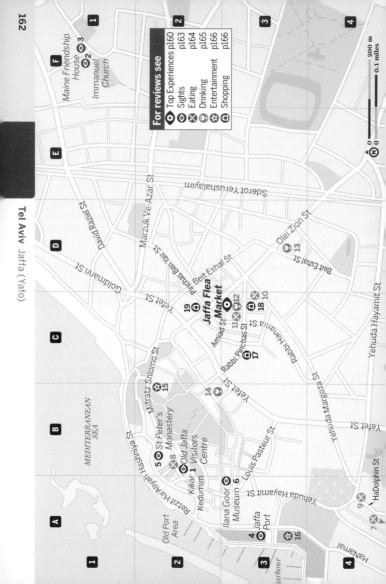

MEDITERRANEAN SEA

Old Port Area

Maine Friendship House

Immanuel Church

For reviews see

◉ Top Experiences p160
◉ Sights p163
✕ Eating p164
🍷 Drinking p165
🎭 Entertainment p166
🛍 Shopping p166

David Raziel St

Goldmann St

Marzuk Ve-Azar St

Pinchas Ben Yair St

Beit Eshal St

Yefet St

Sderot Yerushalayim

Olei Zion St

Beit Eshal St

Yefet St

Jaffa Flea Market

Amiad St

Rabbi Pinchas St

Rabbi Hanania St

Yehuda Margoza St

Yehuda Hayamit St

Retzif Ha'Aliyah Hashniya St

Mifratz Shlomo St

St Peter's Monastery

Old Jaffa Visitors Centre

Kikar Kedumim

Ilana Goor Museum

Jaffa Port

Louis Pasteur St

Yehuda Hayamit St

Yefet St

HaNamal

HaDolphin St

200 m
0.1 miles

N

Sights

Old Jaffa Visitors Centre
ARCHAEOLOGICAL SITE

1 ⊙ MAP P162, B2

Sometimes called 'Jaffa Tales', this small visitor's centre is actually an archaeological excavation site in a chamber underneath Kedumim Sq. Here, you can view partially excavated remains from the Hellenistic and Roman era and learn about more than 4000 years of Jaffa's colourful history in a virtual experience. (☎ 03-603-7686, 03-603-7000; www.oldjaffa.co.il; Kedumim Sq; adult/student 30/15NIS; ⊙ 9am-8pm Sat-Thu, to 5pm Fri summer, 9am-5pm Sat-Thu, to 3pm Fri winter)

Immanuel Church
CHURCH

2 ⊙ MAP P162, F1

This small but charming German Templer church, now Lutheran, dates from 1904. Its fine organ is used for concerts. Completely unlike anything else in Tel Aviv, it's a little piece of European Christian architecture in the Middle East. It holds services at 11am on Saturday and 10am on Sunday. (www.immanuelchurch-jaffa.com; 15 Be'er Hofman St; ⊙ 10am-2pm Tue-Fri)

Maine Friendship House
MUSEUM

3 ⊙ MAP P162, F1

The first neighbourhood outside Jaffa's city walls, the American Colony was established by a group of American Christians in the

Tel Aviv – Jaffa (Yafo)

View of Jaffa Port (p164)

1860s. You'll learn the engaging story of their star-crossed (some would say hare-brained) settlement scheme at the Maine Friendship House museum. The colony area, run-down but charming, is centred on the corner of Auerbach and Be'er Hoffman Sts, 1km northeast of Jaffa's old city. (☎03-681-9225; www.jaffacolony. com; 10 Auerbach St; ☯noon-3pm Fri, 2-4pm Sat)

Jaffa Port   PORT

4 ◉ MAP P162, A3

One of the oldest known harbours in the world, the port of Jaffa was mentioned in the Bible (as Joppa) and was once the disembarkation point for pilgrims to the Holy Land. Up until recent decades, it was also where Jaffa oranges were stored and exported all over the world. These days it's predominantly an entertainment facility incorporating a boardwalk and warehouses hosting bars, fish restaurants, shops and the not-for-profit Nalaga'at Centre (p166), home to a deaf-blind theatre company. (www.namalyafo. co.il; ☯10am-10pm Mon-Wed, to 11pm Thu, 9am-11pm Fri & Sat; 🅿; 🚌Dan 10, 18, 25, 41)

St Peter's Monastery   CHURCH

5 ◉ MAP P162, B2

The most prominent building in Jaffa, this beautiful cream-painted Franciscan church was built in the 1890s on the ruins of the Crusader citadel and is still used as a place

of worship. In December it's one of the few places in town where you'll find a giant Christmas tree. (Kedumim Sq; ☯8-11.45am & 3-5pm Oct-Feb, to 6pm Mar-Sep)

Ilana Goor Museum   GALLERY

6 ◉ MAP P162, A3

Built in the 18th century, this imposing stone building just south of Kedumim Sq originally served as a hostel for Jewish pilgrims arriving at Jaffa and was later converted into a soap and perfume factory. Now the residence of local artist Ilana Goor, it is open to the public as a gallery. The collection here won't be to all tastes, being dominated by tribal art and works by Goor, but the interior spaces and panoramic terrace are extremely attractive. (☎03-683-7676; www. ilanagoormuseum.org; 4 Mazal Dagim St; adult/student/child 30/25/20NIS; ☯10am-4pm Sun-Fri, to 5pm Sat; 🚌Dan 10, 18, 25, 41)

Eating

Old Man & the Sea   SEAFOOD $$$

7 ✖ MAP P162, A4

As classic as the Hemingway novel of the same name, this Old Man is still at the top of its game. Spacious enough for dozens of waiters to serve hundreds of people, its terrace overlooks the sea in southern Jaffa. Huge portions of fish or seafood come with 20 or so small mezze, such as falafel balls and hummus. (☎03-681-8699; 85 Kedem St; mains from 84NIS; ☯11am-1am)

Kalamata

GREEK $$

8 ✖ MAP P162, B2

A real Tel Aviv *taverna*, this cute restaurant, set in a 500-year-old house on the main tourist square, offers a predominantly Greek and Cypriot menu but with a Middle Eastern twist. Every dish here is delicious, but tasty starters include stuffed vine leaves and Arab-style ceviche; mains range from black seafood pasta to lamb or fish kebabs. (☏03-681-9998; www.kalamata.co.il; 10 Kedumim Sq; mains from 62NIS; ☺5pm-late Sun-Wed, from noon Thu-Sat; ☎)

Ali Caravan

MIDDLE EASTERN $

9 ✖ MAP P162, A4

If hummus is a religion, then Ali Caravan could well be its Mecca. This tiny restaurant near Jaffa Port offers a limited menu of three hummus choices: plain, *fuul* (with mashed and spiced fava beans) or *masabacha* (with chickpeas and warm tahina). It's always busy, so you'll probably have to queue. (Abu Hassan, 1 HaDolphin St; hummus 20NIS; ☺8am-3pm Sun-Fri; ⚲; 🚌Dan 10, 18, 25, 41)

Puaa

CAFE $$

10 ✖ MAP P162, C3

The thrift-shop-chic decor is truly authentic here – every piece of furniture and every decorative knicknack is for sale. In the midst of the flea-market action, laid-back Puaa serves an all-day breakfast and is particularly busy on weekends. (☏03-682-3821; www.puaa.co.il; 8 Rabbi Yohanan St; mains 46-76NIS; ☺9am-1am Sun-Fri, from 10am Sat; ☎; 🚌Dan 10, 18, 25, 41)

Onza

MEDITERRANEAN $$

11 ✖ MAP P162, C3

Onza taps into the buzz of the Jaffa flea market with its lively atmosphere of music, cocktails and gourmet food. Influenced by the Ottoman-era architecture here, the menu includes Turkish kebabs, mezze starters and breads baked in the Middle Eastern taboun oven, plus seafood caught by local fishers. A good spot for a drink or two. (☏03-648-6060; www.onza.co.il; 3 Rabbi Hanania St; mains 42-106NIS; ☺6pm-midnight; ☎)

Drinking

Shaffa Bar

CAFE

12 ☕ MAP P162, C3

Another hipster hangout (Jaffa is full of them), Shaffa is a favourite among the cafe-bar hybrids in the flea market for its unpretentious vibe and range of well-executed eats. The coffee machine and cocktail shaker get an equal workout, and it's possible to order everything from a simple sandwich to a crunchy Thai salad or comfort food, like Irish sausages. (☏03-681-1205; 3 Rabbi Nachman St; ☺9am-late; ☎; 🚌Dan 10, 18, 25, 41)

Cuckoo's Nest

BAR

13 🚌 MAP P162, D3

The Cuckoo's Nest (*Ken HaKookia* in Hebrew) is run by the same owners as popular rooftop bar Prince (p142). Like its sister space, it has a rooftop beer garden and regularly holds nights with DJs and live electronic music. (📞054-838-7452; www.facebook.com/Cnestjaffa; 3 Noam St; ⏰7pm-4am)

Beit Kandinof

BAR

14 🚌 MAP P162, B2

Beit Kandinof is both an art education centre and happening bar. Set in an old Ottoman-era building, its painting and drawing classes (in English) run from 6.30pm to 8.30pm. Afterwards the place fills up to become a bar with resident DJs. The food menu offers mezze and Moroccan and Turkish-inspired dishes. (📞03-650-2938; www.facebook.com/beitkandinofyaffo; 14 Hatzorfim St; ⏰5pm-1am Mon-Wed, to 2am Thu, 11am-2am Fri & Sat; 📶)

Entertainment

Jaffa Theatre

THEATRE

15 ⭐ MAP P162, B2

Founded in 1998 in a multiarched Old Jaffa building to bring two cultures together, this stage showcases Hebrew- and Arabic-language plays, sometimes with English translations. Not afraid to run plays that tackle the Israeli-Palestinian conflict, it's an inviting space to glean native insight on complex topics. It also holds musical performances and festivals such as the Arab-Hebrew Women's Festival. (Arab-Hebrew Theatre; 📞03-518-5563; www.arab-hebrew-theatre.org.il; 10 Mifratz Shlomo St)

Nalaga'at Centre

THEATRE

16 ⭐ MAP P162, A3

A unique nonprofit organisation set in a renovated shipping hangar, Nalaga'at (meaning 'Do Touch') is the only deaf-blind theatre company in the world. While watching a show here, it's easy to forget that the people on stage cannot see or hear, as the actors tell stories, play musical instruments and even perform choreographed dances. (📞03-633-0808; www.nalagaat.org.il; Jaffa Port)

Shopping

Saga

DESIGN

17 🔒 MAP P162, C3

This art and design shop features a cleanly curated selection of modern wares, from prints and knick-knacks to jewellery and furniture – all crafted by local Tel Aviv artisans. For the stragglers to Jaffa on a Friday, it's one of the few places that stays open later than most. (📞03-670-6062; www.sagatlv.com; 4 Rabbi Pinchas St; ⏰10am-8pm Sun-Thu, to 4pm Fri, 11am-6pm Sat)

Ilana Goor Museum (p164)

Shelly Dahari   FASHION & ACCESSORIES

18 🔒 MAP P162, C3

Fashionistas head to this boutique in Jaffa's flea market to source premium denim, boho baubles and strikingly unique statement jewellery – all designed and handmade in Tel Aviv. (📱03-620-8004; www. shellydahari.com; 14 Rabbi Pinchas St; ⏰9.30am-8pm Sun-Thu, to 4pm Fri)

Zielinski & Rozen   PERFUME

19 🔒 MAP P162, C2

Planters filled with jasmine adorn the front of this perfumerie, which has the ambience of an old apothecary. Bottles of perfume, room spray and handwash are ready to buy, but the highlight here is picking up a souvenir that will truly linger long after your holiday ends – its possible to formulate your very own personalised fragrance. Book ahead. (📱03-573-3470; www.zrp.co.il; 5 Olei Zion St; ⏰10.30am-6.30pm Sun-Thu, 9.30am-3.30pm Fri; 🚌Dan 10, 18, 25, 41)

Survival Guide

Before You Go

Book Your Stay

o In general, accommodation prices in Jerusalem and Tel Aviv are fairly high. Booking in advance is recommended.

o With over 3.6 million tourists arriving in Israel per year, most of whom visit Jerusalem, hotel rooms fill up quickly – especially in summer. Accommodations range from hostels and high-rise, resort-like hotels with impressive pools to elegant beachside picks, stylish boutique options in historic buildings and B&Bs set in residential neighbourhoods.

o In Tel Aviv, look for charming boutique hotels around Rothschild Blvd. Jaffa, with its vibrant, Arab-inflected street life, also makes for a great base. Hostels can be found near Yehuda HaLevi St, currently being redeveloped for the light rail. Major hotel chains tend to locate their towers overlooking the beach, along busy HaYarkon St.

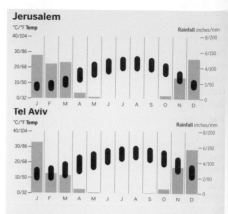

When to Go

April–May Pleasant and sunny, but be prepared for crowds and hefty hotel rates.

July–August Temperatures sizzle when the calendar is packed with festivals and events.

September– October Excellent, mild weather, but Jewish holidays can increase costs.

Useful Websites

iTravel Jerusalem (www.itraveljerusalem. com) City's tourism website; listings include recommendations for pilgrims and families.

Windows of Jerusalem (www.windowsof jerusalem.com) Quality fully furnished apartment rentals.

Isralet (www.isralet. com) Israel-wide service with Jerusalem B&Bs, apartments and other accommodation.

Tel Aviv Hotel Association (www.visit-tel-aviv.com) The official organisation of the city's body of hotels.

Lonely Planet (lonely planet.com/israel-and-the-palestinian-territo ries) Recommendations.

Best Budget

Abraham Hostel (https://abraham

hostels.com) The biggest and one of the best hostels in Tel Aviv.

Post Hostel (http://theposthostel.com) Contemporary stylish digs in a downtown Jerusalem post office.

Old Jaffa Hostel (www.telaviv-hostel.com) Super cool space with ancient charm in the heart of Jaffa.

Stay Inn Hostel (www.stayinhostel.com) Well furnished lounge areas, indoors and out, with spic and span rooms in downtown Jerusalem.

Best Midrange

YMCA Three Arches Hotel (www.ymca3arches.com) Historic architecture and top notch facilities in Jerusalem.

Hashimi Hotel (www.hashimihotel.com) Clean, basic rooms but extraordinary Old City views.

Dave West TLV (http://brownhotels.com/dave) Funky art and vintage design pick near Gordon Beach.

Port Hotel (www.porthoteltelaviv.com) Rooftop terrace and beach proximity without

exorbitant rates – a rarity in Tel Aviv indeed.

Best Top End

King David Hotel (https://www3.danhotels.com/Jerusalem Hotels/KingDavid JerusalemHotel) Grand art-deco retreat, one of Jerusalem's most iconic.

Rothschild Hotel (www.rothschild-hotel.co.il) A veteran among Tel Aviv's boutique picks, the stellar service is above the rest.

American Colony Hotel (www.americancolony.com) Old-world posh in a former pasha's palace in East Jerusalem.

Arriving in Jerusalem & Tel Aviv

Ben Gurion International Airport

○ **Ben Gurion International Airport** (www.iaa.gov.il), 22km from Tel Aviv and 52km from Jerusalem, is the country's gateway for international flights.

○ Airport security is very tight, so if you're flying internationally, check in at least three hours before your flight when flying both to and from Israel.

Allenby Crossing (King Hussein Bridge)

○ It's possible to travel overland from Jordan to Jerusalem via the Allenby Bridge crossing point (known as King Hussein Bridge in Jordan) only 30km to the east of the city.

○ Jordanian visas are not available on arrival and must be obtained in advance at a Jordanian embassy or by purchasing the Jordan Pass (www.jordanpass.jo) online.

○ Departure taxes are charged, passport and visa checks are rigorous, and security checks (especially on the Israeli side) can add hours to the journey time.

○ The crossing point is open from 8am to midnight Sunday to Thursday, and to noon on Friday and Saturday. It closes on Jewish and Muslim holidays.

Getting Around

Bicycle

o The quickest and easiest way to travel Tel Aviv is on a bicycle, thanks in part to 120km of dedicated bike paths along thoroughfares such as Rothschild Blvd, Chen Blvd, Ben-Gurion Blvd and Ibn Gabirol St.

o For epic rides, go to **Park HaYarkon** (Ganei Yehoshua; Map p150; www.park.co.il; Rokach Blvd; P) and head east, or pedal along the 10km coastal promenade. For bike hire, try **O-Fun** (📞03-544-2292; http://ofun.co.il; 197 Ben Yehuda St; per hr/24hr/weekend 25/75/130NIS; ⏱9.30am-7pm Sun-Thu, to 2pm Fri) on Ben Yehuda St or the other branch of **O-Fun** (📞03-522-0488; http://ofun.co.il; 32 Allenby St; ⏱10am-7pm Sun-Thu, to 2pm Fri) on Allenby St.

o With many steep areas and a hectic downtown, Jerusalem is best suited to experienced cyclists. **Bike Jerusalem** (📞02-579-6353; www.bikejerusalem.com; hire per day from 70NIS) offers rental bikes with downtown pick-up (including helmet and repair kit), while **Smart Tour** (📞02-561-8056; https://smart-tour.co.il; 4 David Remez St, First Station; regular/electric bike per day 99/199NIS; ⏱9am-6pm Sun-Thu, to 12.30pm Fri) takes some of the effort out of pedalling the city hills by offering electric-bike rental.

Bus

o Jerusalem is laced with a good network of bus routes (5.90NIS per ride), which cover all West Jerusalem neighbourhoods (and reach into a few in East Jerusalem). Buy a rechargeable Rav-Kav card from any driver or the convenient Jerusalem City Pass – slide the card into the machine next to the driver upon entering (there's a 90-minute window for free transfer between buses and the light-rail line with the card). You cannot buy a single ride fare from bus drivers.

o Tel Aviv city buses are operated by the Dan cooperative (www.dan.co.il) and follow an efficient network of routes, from 5.30am to midnight, except on Shabbat. A ticket for a single ride costs 6.90NIS, a one-day pass (hofshi yomi) allowing unlimited bus travel around Tel Aviv and its suburbs costs 13.50NIS and a weekly card (hofshi shavoui) costs 64NIS.

Car & Motorcycle

In Jerusalem, traffic congestion is common, one-way streets are a headache, some roads are barely wide enough to pass, drivers are impatient, and parking is painful – consider carefully whether you need a car.

Paid street parking available to non-residents is marked by a blue-and-white kerb; purchase a ticket from a nearby machine (5.70NIS per hour) and display it on your dashboard.

Street parking is usually free in the evening and during Shabbat. Alternatively, register with Pango (http://en.pango.co.il) to locate available spaces and pay for parking through an app on your phone (in some places, your only option is to pay through Pango). Parking fines are applied readily, and cars are towed swiftly if illegally parked.

Driving in the Old City is prohibited. For convenient and secure parking near Jaffa Gate, head to **Mamilla Parking** (17 Kariv St; 1st hour free, each subsequent hour 12NIS, full day 50NIS; ⏰6am-2am), or park at the First Station complex and from there grab the free **shuttle service** (☎02-329-0758; www.itraveljerusalem.com/ent/free-ride-old-city-shuttle-service-first-station; ⏰8am-8pm Sun, Tue & Wed, 7am-8pm Mon & Thu, 8am-1pm Fri) to the Old City.

In Tel Aviv, street parking can be very difficult. Cars are only allowed to park in spaces with blue-and-white kerbs. Most streets require payment during the day (6.20NIS per hour) and are reserved for residents from 5pm to 9am.

Among the complicating factors: the yellow signs that explain the rules that apply to the side of the street they're on may not be in English. Parking next to a red-and white kerb is illegal – if you park in one of these spaces your car *will* be towed.

Privately owned car parks and garages (often signposted with electronic information on whether they're full) charge upwards of 60NIS per 24 hours.

Public car parks charge considerably less (usually a flat rate of 20NIS from 7am to 7pm, or 8NIS to 10NIS per hour). There are conveniently located large public car parks in front of the **Old Railway Station** (HaTachana; www.hatachana.co.il; Neve Tzedek; ⏰10am-10pm Sat-Thu, to 5pm Fri; 🅿; 🚌18, 10, 100) on Herbert Samuel Promenade and just south of **Jaffa Port** (Map p162; www.namalyafo.co.il; ⏰10am-10pm Mon-Wed, to 11pm Thu, 9am-11pm Fri & Sat; 🅿, 🚌Dan 10, 18, 25, 41).

The city's biggest car park is the **Reading Terminal** (15 Rokach Blvd), on the outskirts of Tel Aviv near Park HaYarkon. Because of its location and good bus connections, it's often used as a 'park and ride' option.

Parking on Shabbat (Friday evening to Saturday afternoon) is usually a bit easier as many Tel Avivians

leave the city on day trips, and most car parks are open. Useful car parks are located on Ben Saruk St (near Arlozorov St), Sarona (Kaplan St), Basel St and Habima (Rothschild Blvd).

Most of the main car-rental agencies have offices on HaYarkon St.

Sherut

Sheruts (shared taxis) depart more frequently than buses and often cost only a few shekels more; on Shabbat they're the only public transport to destinations in Israel.

o In Jerusalem, **sheruts for Tel Aviv** (per person weekday/night/weekend 25/27/35NIS) depart from the corner of Ha'Rav Kook St and Jaffa Rd, near Zion Sq; once in Tel Aviv, they stop just outside the Central Bus Station.

o Jerusalem-bound sheruts (26-36NIS) depart from Tsemach David St outside Tel Aviv's **Central Bus Station** (☎03-638-4112; 108 Levinsky St).

o From **Ben Gurion International Airport** (www.iaa.gov.il), there are sheruts to Jerusalem (from 42NIS). The ticket price is the same on weekdays and Shabbat and includes up to two suitcases.

Taxi

o Taking a 'special' (speshel; ie non-shared) taxi can be very convenient but, at times, a bit of a hassle because some unscrupulous drivers overcharge tourists. The best way to avoid getting ripped off is to sound like a confident old hand as you give the street address, including a cross street.

o It's almost always to your advantage to use the meter (by law the driver has to put it on if you ask); make sure it is reset to the flag-fall price after you get in.

o Meter fall is usually 12.30NIS. Between 9pm and 5.30am and on Shabbat and Jewish holidays, the meter fall begins around 15.30NIS. Wait time costs 94NIS per hour. Legitimate surcharges include pick-up at Ben Gurion Airport (5NIS); pieces of full-size luggage (4.40NIS); third and fourth passengers (4.90NIS each); and phone orders (5.20NIS).

o Taxis operate according to two tariffs: the lower tariff between 5.30am and 9pm and the 25% higher night tariff between 9pm and 5.30am, and on Shabbat and Jewish holidays.

o In Jerusalem, plan on spending between 25NIS and 50NIS for trips anywhere within the central part of town. Ask for a receipt at the end. In Tel Aviv, it's usually 40NIS to 50NIS for most trips within the central city.

o The most popular taxi app is Gett Taxi (https://gett.com), followed by Raxi (www.raxi.com). In Jerusalem, you can also call **Hapalmach Taxi** (☏02-679-3333), or find taxi services by neighbourhood (and sample fares) on JerusalemTaxis (http://jerusalemtaxies.com).

o Drivers at Jaffa Gate are notorious for refusing to use the meter and then overcharging or agreeing on a price and then trying to renegotiate once you're in the cab – if you need a taxi from this location, ask the nearby **tourist office** (☏02-627-1422; www.itraveljerusalem.com;

Jaffa Gate; ◷8.30am-5pm Sat-Thu, to 1.30pm Fri) to call one for you. Drivers waiting next to the Tomb of the Virgin Mary on the Mount of Olives have a similarly bad reputation. If you don't want to get ripped off, you can always make the short walk up the hill to Lions' Gate in the Old City.

Train

o Jerusalem Light Rail (JLR; www.citypass.co.il) consists of a single line with 23 stops, running from Mt Herzl in the west of the city to Heyl HaAvir in Pisgat Ze'ev, in the city's far northeast. Tickets (5.90NIS per ride) can be purchased from the machines at tram stops and must be validated aboard the tram (inspectors frequently check tickets).

o In Tel Aviv, if you need to get from north to south, you can opt to use Israel Railways – there are four stations along the eastern edge of the city: **Savidor** (Arlozorov (Mercaz) Station), **HaHagana**, **HaShalom** (10 Givat HaTahmoshet St) and **University**. Single-journey fares start at 6NIS.

Essential Information

Accessible Travel

○ Not surprisingly for an ancient city, parts of Jerusalem present problems for travellers with mobility issues. Stairs, paving stones and narrow lanes make some areas very difficult to navigate in a wheelchair. However, the Old City, after a many years-long renovation project is now equipped with **4km of wheelchair accessible alleyways** in the Muslim, Christian (including the **Via Dolorosa**) and Armenian quarters. And a free app called Accessible JLM-Old City, available in seven languages helps users map out a navigable route to all the major sites.

○ Several top sights are accessible to travellers with a disability, including almost all parts of the **Yad Vashem** (p102) complex and the **Israel Museum** (p92) – both have parking and toilets for visitors with disabilities, too; the **Garden Tomb** (p68) in East Jerusalem has accessibility ramps.

○ There is smooth asphalt leading to **Jaffa Gate** (p50), and (relatively) flat paving in the immediate area around the **Tower of David** (p48; its sound-and-light show includes audio-guided descriptions for the visually impaired, and the Time Elevator can accommodate visitors with disabilities).

○ You can approach the **Western Wall** (p42) plaza from Dung Gate without stairs.

○ **Temple Mount/Al Haram Ash Sharif** (p34) is accessed by a long covered ramp, and at the site there are only a few stairs to reach the **Dome of the Rock** (p35).

○ The **Church of the Holy Sepulchre** (p38) has an entrance ramp, though many of the shrines inside are only reachable by stairs.

○ Many Jerusalem restaurants are on roof terraces, up stairs or tucked into alleys, but **Mamilla Mall** is a pedestrianised shopping centre lined with cafes and restaurants at ground level. The **tourist office** (p174) can provide additional advice on suitable restaurants and bars.

○ Tel Aviv's central seafront boardwalk has been redeveloped and offers wheelchair access to **Hilton** (p152) and **Frishman** (p157) beaches

○ The **Old Port** (p152) has a wide deck offering sea views and lots of restaurants, plus the **Nalaga'at Centre** (p166) in Jaffa is an inspirational deaf-blind theatre.

○ An app called Step-Hear for the visually impaired (available in Arabic, English and Hebrew, with more languages to come) offers voice-guided tours of the Old City.

○ For more details on disabled access, go to the Access Israel website (www.aisrael.org).

Business Hours

Opening hours for tourist attractions may be reduced by an hour or more in winter, but almost all museums, restaurants and hotels open year-round. Most businesses close for Shabbat, from Friday afternoon until Saturday evening, though some non-Jewish-run businesses remain open. In Tel Aviv, cafes and bars stay open late over the weekend.

Banks 9am–1pm Sunday–Friday, plus 4pm–6pm Monday–Thursday

Restaurants 11am–11pm Sunday–Thursday, to 1pm Friday, from 9pm Saturday

Museums 10am–6pm Sunday to Thursday, to 2pm on Friday, some open on Saturday

Shops 9am–6pm Sunday–Thursday, to 2pm Friday

Bars 6pm–late

Clubs 11pm–4am Thursday–Sunday

COVID-19

Throughout the COVID-19 pandemic Israel has placed strict restrictions on non-Israeli international travellers from entering the country. During various surges in infections, entry has been shut off entirely. Check the Israeli Ministry of Health coronavirus website for the latest information: https://corona.health.gov.il/en/.

Discount Cards

○ An International Student Identity Card (ISIC)

doesn't get anywhere near as many discounts as it once did – none, for instance, are available on public transport; however, you can get 25% off **Sandemans New Jerusalem Tours** (www.newjerusalemtours.com; ⏱11am, 2pm & 5pm).

○ The Jerusalem City Pass offers discounts of 20% to 50% at more than a dozen sights and museums.

○ The Secret Tel Aviv community, a local events website with a popular Facebook group, offers a free VIP card (www.secrettelaviv.com/vip-card) that'll score you discounts on restaurants, bars, shops, tours and more. Sign up online and collect it from one of the permanent pick-up locations, such as **Cafe Xoho** (☎072-249-5497; www.cafexoho.com; 17 Gordon St; mains from 42NIS; ⏱8am-6.30pm Sun & Tue-Thu, to 4.30pm Fri, 9am-5.30pm Sat; 🛜).

○ A Hostelling International (HI) card is useful for discounts at official HI hostels.

○ Some museums and sights offer discounts to senior citizens, though

to qualify you may not only need to be senior but also a citizen.

Electricity

Type C
230V/50Hz

Type H
230V/50Hz

Insurance

It's always a good idea to take out a travel insurance policy before leaving home. In addition to the usual coverage for sickness (visiting an emergency room/casualty ward can be expensive) and theft, make sure that your coverage is appropriate for your specific needs. For instance, if you plan to scuba dive, skydive or ski, make sure your policy covers these activities. Almost all policies exclude liabilities caused by 'acts of war'.

Even as a tourist, it's possible to get pretty complete medical coverage at reasonable rates through one of Israel's excellent HMOs, provided you'll be staying for at least three to six months. For details, drop by one of the offices of these organisations:

Maccabi Healthcare Services (www.maccabi4u.co.il) Look for details on its Welcome program.

Me'uchedet (www.meuhedet.co.il) Provides coverage under its Foreign Members Plan.

Money

ATMs

You'll have no problem finding ATMs, but as they aren't refilled on Friday night or on Saturday during Shabbat, they sometimes run out of cash at those times. Banks have sporadic opening hours and generally higher commission rates than the exchange bureaus.

Bargaining

Most of your bargaining experiences will happen in the Old City and Jaffa souqs, flea markets or in taxis. While taxi drivers are required by law to use a meter, they rarely miss the chance to fleece tourists for a few shekels; particular spots, such as at the base of the Mount of Olives, are especially notorious. As with bargaining across the world, it pays to keep your cool and – particularly with souvenirs – remember that as the buyer you ultimately have the advantage.

Changing Money

In Jerusalem, the best deals for changing money are at the private, commission-free exchange offices in the downtown area (around Zion Sq and on Ben Hillel St), East Jerusalem (Salah Ad Din St) and in the Old City (Jaffa Gate). In Jewish areas, many close early on Friday and remain closed all day Saturday.

If you're seeking exchange bureaus in Tel Aviv, you'll find no shortage on Allenby, Ibn Gabirol and Dizengott Sts. Most are open from 9am to 9pm Sunday to Thursday, and until 2pm on Friday.

Taxes & Refunds

Israel has value added tax (VAT) of 17% included in all purchases. Israeli citizens have to pay VAT when staying in hotels and hiring cars, but tourists are exempt. Accommodation prices given in shekels include VAT, so most places (though not some B&Bs) charge non-Israelis significantly less than their shekel prices. Prices given in

Tipping

While not typically expected, tipping is increasingly common.

Restaurants Waiters will expect a tip, 10% to 15% is fair.

Pubs Usually have tip jars on the bar; 10% to 15% of your bill is a good amount.

Guides It's good to tip guides: 10NIS to 20NIS is fair.

Hotels 10NIS to 20NIS a night for housekeeping is a nice touch.

Taxis Round up the price of the fare.

US dollars, and those generated by hotel-booking websites, do not include VAT so Israeli citizens will find an extra 17% tacked on at checkout.

Post

Letters and postcards sent with Israel Post (www.israelpost.co.il) to North America and Australasia take seven to 10 days to arrive; to Europe it's a bit less. Incoming mail takes three or four days from Europe and around a week from other places; packages are much slower.

For express service, options include DHL (www.dhl.co.il) and UPS (www.ups.com); Israel Post's EMS (Express Mail Service) is cheaper but slower and not as reliable.

Public Holidays

Between the myriad Jewish and Muslim festivals and holy days that are marked (both officially and unofficially), it can often feel like there is a rarely a day in the calendar that isn't some sort of national holiday.

During Jewish holidays such as Passover, most restaurants, bars and even supermarkets will close in religious areas, while Yom Kippur makes travelling by road anywhere in the country virtually impossible.

As well as the religious holidays, there are a number of national holidays that can have an impact on your stay.

Holocaust Memorial Day Yom HaSho'ah is a solemn remembrance of the six million Jews, including 1.5 million children, who died in the Holocaust. Places of entertainment are closed. At 10am sirens sound and Israelis stand silently at attention wherever they happen to be (17–18 April 2023, 4–5 May 2024, 24–25 April 2025).

Memorial Day Commemorates soldiers who fell defending Israel and the victims of terrorism. Places of entertainment are closed. At 8pm and 11am sirens sound and Israelis stand silently at attention wherever they happen to be. Falls on the day before Israel Independence Day (24–25 April 2023, 12–13 May, 2024, 29–30 April 2025).

Israel Independence Day Ha'Atzma'ut celebrates Israel's declaration of independence in 1948. Marked with official ceremonies, public celebrations with live music, picnics and hikes (25–26 April 2023, 13–14 May 2025, 30 April–1 May 2025).

Yom Kippur The Jewish Day of Atonement is a solemn day of reflection and fasting – and cycling on the empty roads. In Jewish areas, all businesses shut and transport (including by private car) completely ceases; Israel's airports and land borders also close (4–5 October 2022, 24–25 September 2023, 11–12 October 2024).

Hanukkah During the Jewish Festival of Lights, expect Shabbat-like closures on the first and last days only. Some Israelis go on holiday, so accommodation is scarce and room prices rise (18–26 December 2022, 7–15 December 2023, 25 December 2024–2 January 2025).

Safe Travel

Most travellers to Jerusalem enjoy their visit without incident, but be cautious: ongoing tensions can escalate quickly, sometimes violently. Some people feel anxious seeing so many heavily-armed uniformed border police in the Old City streets.

○ Demonstrations by Jews and Arabs are common. Many are peaceful, but steer clear of protests. Damascus Gate, Lions' Gate and Temple Mount/Al Haram Ash Sharif are common flashpoints.

○ Many travellers report feeling unwelcome around the Mount of Olives, and some women travellers have reported harassment. If possible, don't visit alone.

○ Ultra-Orthodox Jewish groups sometimes stone vehicles and violently confront the police in the neighbourhood of Mea She'arim. Hostilities can also erupt when tourists (especially those deemed to be immodestly dressed) saunter in.

Tel Aviv is a remarkably safe city. Despite the sometimes harrowing headlines, including a shooting in Sarona Market (2016), rockets being fired from Gaza (2012 and 2014) and suicide attacks (during the Second Intifada), Tel Avivians are generally unperturbed by the threat of terrorism. The streets are safe to walk at all times of the day and night, and theft from public areas is rare.

○ Public underground bomb shelters (*miklat*) are scattered over the city, usually in parks.

○ In the extremely rare event of an air-raid siren, go to the fortified room (*mamad*) or stairwell of a building.

Toilets

Toilet facilities in Jerusalem and Tel Aviv, including public toilets in the Old City, are very good. Nearly all are Western style.

Tourist Information

The Jerusalem Tourism Authority's official website (www.itraveljerusalem.com) is a great source of information

Jaffa Gate Tourist Office (p174) Main tourist office for Jerusalem. It supplies free maps, organises guides and provides information and advice. It's the second office after Jaffa Gate.

Tourist Information Office (📞 03-516-6188; www.visit-tel-aviv.com; 46 Herbert Samuel Esplanade;

Dos & Don'ts

Unsurprisingly, Israel can feel like a bit of a minefield when it comes to etiquette – even in liberal Tel Aviv. A few tactics can help prevent offending sensibilities.

Avoid politics Unless you know someone well, it pays to avoid expressing an opinion on the conflict; consider your audience when doing so.

Be polite Even if it feels like nobody else is! Israelis are famously brusque, so don't be surprised if interactions don't come with Ps and Qs.

Dress accordingly Important in Orthodox Jewish or Arab neighbourhoods. In buses and sheruts, a woman sitting next to an ultra-Orthodox Jewish man may make him uncomfortable. Depending on how you look at it, that's either his problem or a local sensitivity you should respect.

⊘ 9.30am-5.30pm Sun-Thu, to 1pm Fri Nov-Mar, to 6.30pm Sun-Thu, to 2pm Apr-Oct) Main tourist office for Tel Aviv. Staff provide maps, brochures and plenty of advice.

Jaffa Tourist Information Office (☏ 03-516-6188; www.visit-tel-aviv.com; 2 Marzuk Ve-Azar St; ⊘ 9.30am-5.30pm Sun-Thu, to 1pm Fri, 10am-4pm Sat Apr-Oct, 9.30am-5.30pm Sun-Thu, 9am-2pm Fri Nov-Mar) Recommendations and a free Jaffa map near the clock tower.

Responsible Travel

Being a thoughtful visitor in a destination fraught with religious, political and cultural conflicts means doing some research in advance. Try to best plan your trip to align with whatever values you prioritise, but curiosity and openness to a variety of voices and perspectives will allow you to learn and discover the most. Always be respectful of cultural and religious mores, including the dress code when visiting places of worship in Jerusalem. Tel Aviv, on the other hand, is decidedly more casual.

In a country already vulnerable to the impacts of climate change, especially chronic water shortages (most easily visible in the Dead Sea's receding shoreline and the decreasing flow of the Jordan River) it's best to always limit your water usage as much as possible. This might simply mean taking quick showers or staying in hotels, hostels, kibbutzim or home stays that prioritise sustainable water use.

Staying with Jerusalemites in their homes is a great way to experience local communities and culture. One new initiative, Women and Stories in Jerusalem (www.women-jerusalem.com), offers visitors homestays, meals, tours and workshops from women, mostly artists and craftspeople, who have chosen to share their lives and stories with visitors from abroad.

Language

Hebrew is the national language of Israel, with seven to eight million speakers worldwide. It's written from right to left in its own alphabet.

Read our coloured pronunciation guides as if they were English and you'll be understood. Most sounds have equivalents in English. Note that *a* is pronounced as 'ah', *ai* as in 'aisle', *e* as in 'bet', *i* as the 'ea' in 'heat', *o* as 'oh' and *u* as the 'oo' in 'boot'. Both *kh* (like the 'ch' in the Scottish *loch*) and *r* (similar to the French 'r') are guttural sounds pronounced at the back of the throat. The apostrophe (') indicates the glottal stop (like the pause in the middle of 'uh oh'). The stressed syllables are indicated with *italics*.

To enhance your trip with a phrasebook, visit **lonelyplanet.com**.

Basics

Hello.	שלום.	sha·lom
Goodbye.	להתראות.	le·hit·ra·ot
Yes.	כן	ken
No.	לא.	lo
Please.	בבקשה.	be·va·ka·sha
Thank you.	תודה.	to·da
Excuse me./ Sorry.	סליחה.	sli·kha

How are you?
מה נשמע?   ma nish·ma

Fine, thanks. And you?
טוב, תודה.   tov to·da
ואתה/ואת?   ve·a·ta/ve·at (m/f)

What's your name?
איך קוראים לך?   ekh kor·im le·kha/lakh (m/f)

My name is ...
שמי ...   shmi ...

Do you speak English?
אתה מדבר אנגלית?   a·ta me·da·ber ang·lit (m)
את מדברת אנגלית?   at me·da·be·ret ang·lit (f)

I don't understand.
אני לא מבין/מבינה.   a·ni lo me·vin/ me·vi·na (m/f)

Eating & Drinking

Can you recommend a ...?
אתה יכול להמליץ על...?   a·ta ya·khol le·ham·lit·sal (m)
את יכולה להמליץ על...?   at ye·cho·la le·ham·lit·sal...(f)

cafe	בית קפה	bet ka·fe
restaurant	מסעדה	mis·a·da

What would you recommend?
מה אתה ממליץ?   ma a·ta mam·lits (m)
מה את ממליצה?   ma at mam·li·tsa (f)

What's the local speciality?
מה המאכל המקומי?   ma ha·ma·'a·khal ha·me·ko mi

Do you have vegetarian food?
יש לכם אוכל   yesh la·khem o·khel
צמחוני?   tsim·kho·ni

I'd like the ..., please.
אני צריך/   a·ni tsa·rikh/
צריכה את   tsri·kha et
..., בבקשה.   ... be·va·ka·sha (m/f)

bill	החשבון	ha·khesh·bon
menu	התפריט	ha·taf·rit

Numbers

1	אחת	a·khat
2	שתיים	shta·yim
3	שלוש	sha·losh
4	ארבע	ar·ba
5	חמש	kha·mesh
6	שש	shesh
7	שבע	she·va
8	שמונה	shmo·ne
9	תשע	te·sha
10	עשר	e·ser
100	מאה	me·a
1000	אלף	e·lef

Note that English numerals are used in modern Hebrew text.

Emergencies

Help!	הצילו!	ha·tsi·lu
Go away!	לך מפה!	lekh mi·po
Call ...!	תתקשר ל...!	tit·ka·sher le ...
a doctor	רופא	ro·fe/ro·fa (m/f)
the police	משטרה	mish·ta·ra

I'm lost.

אני אבוד.   a·ni a·vud (m)
אני אבודה.   a·ni a·vu·da (f)

Where are the toilets?

איפה השירותים?   e·fo ha·she·ru·tim

I'm sick.

אני חולה.   a·ni kho·le/kho·la (m/f)

Transport & Directions

Is this the ... to (Haifa)?
האם זה/ זאת ה ... ל·(חיפה)?   ha·im ze/ zot ha ... le·(khai·fa) (m/f)

boat	אוניה	o·ni·ya (f)
bus	אוטובוס	o·to·bus (m)
plane	מטוס	ma·tos (m)
train	רכבת	ra·ke·vet (f)

One ... ticket, please.
כרטיס ... אחד בבקשה.   kar·tis e·khad ... be·va·ka·sha

| one way | לכיוון אחד | le·ki·vun e·khad |
| return | הלוך ושוב | ha·lokh va·shov |

How much is it to ...?
כמה זה ל...?   ka·ma ze le ...

Please take me to (this address).
תיקח/תיקחי אותי ל·(כתובת הזאת) בבקשה.   ti·kakh/tik·khi o·ti (lak·to·vet ha·zot) be·va·ka·sha (m/f)

Where's the (market)?
איפה ה (שוק)?   e·fo ha (shuk)

Can you show me (on the map)?
אתה/את יכול/יכולה להראות לי (על המפה)?   a·ta/at ya·khol/ye·kho·la le·har·ot li (al ha·ma·pa) (m/f)

What's the address?
מה הכתובת?   ma hak·to·vet

Behind the Scenes

Send Us Your Feedback

We love to hear from travellers – your comments help make our books better. We read every word, and we guarantee that your feedback goes straight to the authors. Visit **lonelyplanet.com/contact** to submit your updates and suggestions.

Note: We may edit, reproduce and incorporate your comments in Lonely Planet products such as guidebooks, websites and digital products, so let us know if you don't want your comments reproduced or your name acknowledged. For a copy of our privacy policy visit lonelyplanet.com/legal.

MaSovaida's Thanks

Many thanks to the sweet and spirited Tel Avivians for the invaluable tips, insights, and accompaniment – specifically Noa Mescor (and Hailey Mahan for the intro), Roy Itzhack, Gavi Nelson, Tal Lubin, and Aviv Levy and the Jerusalem Computers crew. Thanks to Lauren for the chance to return to this land that I so love.

Michael's Thanks

Just a few of the people who provided advice, assistance and insight into my research and travels in this complex and layered land: Mark Katz, Ellen Shapiro, Eliot Goldstein, Josh Mitnick, Evan Meyer, Yehuda Kaplan, Susanna Dargman, Gura Berger, Ran Lior, Arie Sommers, Flie Nahmias, Imad and Mahmoud Muna.

Acknowledgements

Cover photographs: Front: Azrieli Centre, Tel Aviv; Marco Ferrarin/ Getty Images ©; Back: Western Wall, Jerusalem; StockStudio/ Shutterstock ©

This Book

This 2nd edition of Lonely Planet's *Pocket Jerusalem & Tel Aviv* guidebook was researched and written by MaSovaida Morgan, Michael Grosberg and Anita Isalska. This guidebook was produced by the following:

Senior Product Editors Elizabeth Jones, Angela Tinson

Product Editor Joel Cotterell

Senior Cartographer Valentina Kremenchutskaya

Book Designers Jessica Rose, Lauren Egan

Assisting Editors Melanie Dankel, Gabrielle Innes, Charlotte Orr

Cartographer Hunor Csutoros

Cover Researcher Brendan Dempsey-Spencer

Thanks to Miriam Berger, Carolyn Boicos, Helen Elfer, Sonia Kapoor, Anne Mason, Martine Power, Shuki Rosenboim, Kathryn Rowan, Dan Savery Raz

Index

See also separate subindexes for:

⊗ **Eating** p186
⊙ **Drinking** p187
✪ **Entertainment** p187
🔒 **Shopping** p188

⊙ Shopping

Sights **000**
Map Pages **000**

Our Writers

MaSovaida Morgan

MaSovaida is a travel writer and multimedia storyteller whose wanderlust has taken her to more than 40 countries and all seven continents. Previously, she was Lonely Planet's Destination Editor for South America and Antarctica for four years and worked as an editor for newspapers and NGOs in the Middle East and the United Kingdom. Follow her on Instagram @MaSovaida.

Michael Grosberg

Michael has worked on more than 50 Lonely Planet guidebooks. He has also worked in development on Rota in the western Pacific; in South Africa, where he investigated and wrote about political violence and trained newly elected government representatives; and as a teacher in Quito, Ecuador.

Anita Isalska

Anita is a travel journalist, editor and copywriter. After several merry years as a staff writer and editor – a few of them in Lonely Planet's London office – Anita now works freelance between Australia, the UK and any Alpine chalet with good wi-fi. Anita writes about France, Eastern Europe, Southeast Asia and off-beat travel. Read her stuff on www.anitaisalska.com.

Published by Lonely Planet Global Limited
CRN 554153
2nd edition – Jun 2022
ISBN 978 1 78868 4163
© Lonely Planet 2022   Photographs © as indicated 2022
10 9 8 7 6 5 4 3 2
Printed in Malaysia

Although the authors and Lonely Planet have taken all reasonable care in preparing this book, we make no warranty about the accuracy or completeness of its content and, to the maximum extent permitted, disclaim all liability arising from its use.